Erving Goffman: Observing the Unobserved in Modern Society

GEW Social Sciences, With Hichem Karoui (Ed.)

Global East-West (London)

Copyright © 2025 by GEW Social Sciences, With Hichem Karoui (Ed.)

Collection: Sociology and Sociologists.

Global East-West (London).

All rights reserved.

No portion of this book may be reproduced in any form without written permission from the publisher or author, except as permitted by copyright law.

Contents

Part I: Life and Context   1

1. Beginnings   3
   From Manville to Chicago

2. Finding His Voice   23
   The Shetland Islands and Beyond

3. The Scholar as Outsider   43
   A Complex Relationship With the Discipline

Part II: Major Works and Core Concepts   63

4. The Dramaturgical Perspective   65
   The Social Stage

5. Encounters and Rituals   85
   Social Interaction

6. Stigma and Identity   105
   The "Other" and The "I"

7. Total Institutions   125
   Prisons, Mental Asylums, Barracks, Monasteries, etc.

8. Frame Analysis Interpreting, Organising, and Making Sense	143
9. Gender and Interaction Construction and Consolidation of Gender Roles	161
Part III: Method, Style, and Influence	181
10. The Art of Observation Social Sciences Methods and Research Techniques	183
11. Writing Social Life The Social Scientist's Craft and Rigour	203
12. Interdisciplinary Resonance The Interrelation of Various Fields and Disciplines	223
Part IV: Critical Engagements and Contemporary Relevance	243
13. Critiques and Controversies Pros and Cons	245
14. Goffman in the Digital Age Influence and Continuity Beyond His Time	265
15. Legacy and Future Directions Enduring Relevance	289
16. Last Reflections The Enduring Power of the Interaction Order	309
Primary Works by Erving Goffman	329

Part I: Life and Context

1
Beginnings
From Manville to Chicago

The Early Years in Manville

The particularly intriguing sociological perspective stemming from Manville's unique features shaped the sociologist's formative years. Manville's juxtaposition within New Jersey's industrial landscape created a context which, more than any other place, defined the beginnings of a notable sociologist. His appreciation for the complex relationships between the people and the social world around them has roots in middle-class, diverse, multicultural societies, which celebrate the unique beauty of multicultural societies. Life in Manville was like a social laboratory, which provided the necessary building blocks for his future academic career: mastery of the fundamentals of various disciplines. The collective resilience and cohesion during the economically challenging times that the Manville community endured made a lasting impression and fostered an appreciation for the complexities of human relationships in difficult situations. Manville provided the sociologist with a complex social and cultural puzzle that ultimately inspired his future explorations in social relationships and social order. The attitude of the township reflected a sense of unity among the people by motivating them to work rigorously, which shaped his appreciation for the social dynamics of the community. The community's complex social structure, which included individuals from various social and economic classes, concerned the sociologist and prompted his deep and lasting self-reflection on social inequality and its impact on human relationships.

ERVING GOFFMAN: OBSERVING THE UNOB... 5

Through the delicate fabric of time, the young Goffman witnessed the sociocultural tapestry of Manville, New Jersey, which, without a shred of doubt, must have sparked the deep passion he went on to display as a sociologist in the subsequent years.

> Erving Goffman's intellectual and biographical journey—from his early life in **Manville, Alberta (Canada)** to his formative years at the **University of Chicago**—is crucial to understanding the development of his distinctive sociological vision. Though Goffman was famously private and left few personal writings, scholars have reconstructed his intellectual origins through archival work, institutional histories, and contextual analysis.
>
> Key points in this trajectory:
>
> Born in 1922 in **Manville, Alberta**, to Ukrainian-Jewish immigrant parents.
>
> Studied at the **University of Manitoba** (B.A. in sociology and anthropology, 1945).
>
> Served briefly in the Canadian Merchant Navy.
>
> Moved to the **University of Chicago** in 1945–1946, then again in 1949–1953 for graduate work.
>
> At Chicago, he was influenced by (though not formally a student of) **Everett Hughes, W. I. Thomas, Herbert Blumer**, and **Lloyd Warner**—key figures in the **Chicago School of Sociology**.
>
> His fieldwork at **St. Elizabeths Hospital** in Washington, D.C. (1955–1957), conducted under a grant from the National Institute of Mental Health, led to *Asylums* (1961).

Effects of Family and the Environment

In Goffman's case, he had already reached a fairly advanced age of formation when he and his family relocated to Manville from Philadelphia. There was a high probability, regarded as something beyond the shadow of a doubt, that Goffman's journey as a further advancing sociologist had already been greatly determined owing to the influences he was surrounded by within the family and community. Manville, New Jersey, as all would agree, was a veritable pot-pourri of the heady blend of the socio-cultural and the socio-psychological in addition to the socio-political. There was ultimately no escape for Goffman from having to start advancing in the direction Manville had prepared by virtue of the influences he was surrounded by, be it the family or the community. Goffman's family was the driving set of sociologists. He and the family in which he was born, being relatively older, were not in a severe socio-cultural position. In addition, he exhibited a relative ease in the family, which had a comparatively broad outlook towards life. He was essentially of the belief that the outlook, which was somewhat broad, whether of the family or the whole community, would ultimately influence the members of the people and the community, to a great extent, in their years to come.

The town itself left or was likely to have left, if everything Goffman went on to do is to be regarded as his intellectual developments of utopia, and was as influenced as various other forms of geography of the rich cultural or socio-psychological, for that matter, which certainly other subsets of geography of the socio-psychological or the socio-psychological did pay homage to. Manville was beyond doubt where Goffman had reached or ultimately attained while studying to hail the rich geography.

Economic circumstances, community structures, and existing cultural practices were fundamental to his initial understanding of social mechanisms. In addition, the industrial setting of Manville aided Goffman's comprehension of the effects of cities on people, which served as the basis for his later enquiries on urbanism and its relation to the self. In terms of the non-external realities, Goffman's sociology was also shaped greatly by his immediate context. Encounters, social functions, and the mundane activities of life in Manville were a stage for the application of his developing interest in the mechanisms of social life. His social research was built on the deep understanding of the town, and his analysis of social phenomena was centred on aspects of social action and identity performance that were hidden in the context. Manville and family, in addition to the community of the region, were central to shaping the sociology of the young Goffman.

The fundamental crosscurrents of these impact factors initiated the path of academic growth which resulted in his groundbreaking works in the domain of social order and social interaction in the contemporary era.

Educational Background

Manville raised Erving with the utmost regard for the value of education and learning, which remained pivotal during his formative years. Although economically disadvantaged, his family background placed significant value on education and regarded it as a path to social elevation. Curiosity, coupled with an academic inclination, characterised Erving from a very young age, and this was a trait that the schooling system in Manville took advantage of in order to stimulate his passion for sociological inquiry. The education system during his formative years, in a way, stifled his sociological imagination and configured his sociological framework. It was during these years that he developed and refined the foundation of the tools and systems underlying social phenomena. The school systems at this time focused on the development of basic skills such as critical analysis, thinking, and other forms of social interpretation. With school systems that honed in on the boundaries of sociological systems, he tackled the boundaries in areas such as history, literature, and other necessary subjects like the basic sciences. The obstacles were turned into opportunities, which propelled the sociological view towards a more dynamic education. Like so many other young people, he struggled with schoolwork, peer relationships, and the normal problems of growing up. He viewed these problems, however, as valuable lessons that he had to learn in order to develop the determination and resilience to push himself towards self-improvement. His self-prescribed goals eventually drove him to pursue an education that he hoped would change the direction of his life. It was the foundational education he refined early on that led him to pursue the path of sociological inquiry. It was in these treasured places of education that he was able to strengthen his love for learning, develop his critical thinking ability, and ignite his never-ending passion for understanding the complexities of people and their behaviours. Using the sociological principles and the tools he acquired throughout his learning journey, he formed and crystallised the sociological concepts that have defined his work. It was these early years that nurtured the rich sociological inquiry that shaped the mind of one of the greatest sociologists of our age.

The Path to Sociological Inquiry

For E. Goffman, the journey from Manville to the city of Chicago, the centre of learning, was an important part of his early life that helped shape his concern with sociological inquiry.

While Goffman was engaged in other work, he began to develop a profound appreciation for human interactions within a sociological context, which provided the necessary crossroads for him to embark on the studies for which he is commonly known. It was the integration of lessons learnt from school, stories exchanged with others, and, thirdly, personal experiences that moulded the individual in question and served as motivation for understanding the various dimensions of social interactions as well as the relative social interactions and social behaviours. Most importantly, critical experiences and realities from his early life prompted him to reflect, fuelling his intention to investigate the phenomena of human relations and institutional systems. T This was the time when Goffman anticipated beginning his lifelong dedication to striving for and understanding the fine details of human actions, which he viewed as a significant contribution to sociological thinking. For Goffman, the start of this journey instigated a sharp development in his reasoning and, along with that, an appreciation of the deep levels of social and day-to-day life. His lack of discipline and excessive motivation pushed him into a demanding life of social work that did not focus on the individual. As the absence of social reasoning and motivation was readily apparent, Goffman's sociological career was the product of his dedication to understanding the more responsible and profound contexts of human relations.

Within the periods of reflection and activity of a scholar that he was, Goffman observed the beginnings of some of the most important theories and methods that, even today, echo throughout the sociological field. This phase in Goffman's career prepared him for the more intensive sociological explorations he was to undertake later. This in turn gave rise to the sociological career Goffman had, which was devoted to untangling the increasingly complicated sociological elements woven into the social structure of society.

Moving to the City

In the case of Erving Goffman, moving from the small town of Manville in which he grew up to Chicago meant a significant change: the Manville-Chicago shift meant moving into the city. Chicago is known to be a city full of activities, and Goffman was about to see the bright side of that. Chicago's complex social network and activities provided Goffman, who had a sociological mindset, with the opportunities to explore his ideas. While the city was bustling with activity and offered a variety of neighbourhoods, Goffman could be found studying the city's social order in detail. He observed how the social influence of the city changed people's behaviour and how it shaped their identities. Moving into Chicago marked the first important shift in Goffman's life. It was the point at which he began to appreciate the new ideas and sophisticated dimensions of contemporary society and city dwellers.

For Goffman, the transition from the anonymity and physical isolation of city living to the interrelationships found in urban communities represented a distinctly urban experience that refined his thoughts on social roles, interaction rituals, and the management of social impressions. His engagement within the city not only enhanced his sociological imagination with new facets but also set the stage for his revolutionary work around life as theatre. Goffman's exposure to the city resembled a mosaic of diverse social contexts. Along with the dense public areas, there were also private gatherings scattered throughout the city. Each meeting piqued his interest and stimulated his imagination, challenging him to decipher the concealed languages and patterns of social conduct and exchange unique to city life. Through his insightful reflections and observations, Goffman empathetically pieced together the behaviours of city life, becoming increasingly aware of the head and body gestures that accompany social interactions in an urban environment. This shift to urban life also put Goffman in touch with the range of social strata and status relationships as a miniature slice of the social order. He saw the mingling of the socially favoured and disfavoured, the class-ordered city, the urban social imagination, and the self and social identity.

These findings would subsequently shape Goffman's later works on stigma, social order, and the construction of reality as he attempted to distil the essence of urban life into his sociological paradigm. In hindsight, the intersection of his thoughts on urbanism and social interaction catalysed Goffman's gregarious phase. The defining experiences, events, and insights of that period deeply affected his academic career, and he built upon them to become a sociologist of great relevance.

Academic Pursuits at the University of Chicago

Goffman's engagement with the intellectual rigour of the Chicago School permitted the active development of sociological theory and methods. An impressive cast of faculty, renowned for their intellectual and creative innovation, shaped Goffman's education at the Chicago School. He actively participated in seminars, workshops, and scholarly discussions that provided numerous theoretical frameworks and empirical strategies. This decade was a critical period for Goffman in which he expanded the boundaries of many branches of sociology and developed an appreciation for the depth and breadth of social and sociological phenomena. The different branches of study nurtured Goffman's talent for construction and developing diverse perspectives, including the methodological eclecticism that he later exhibited in his research. In his own terms, he claimed that during the period he met a number of different philosophies and methodologies which stimulated his critical thinking. The intellectual fuel that Goffman acquired during his study at Chicago was a powerful driver for his budding ideas and innovations in sociology. He was surrounded by distinguished scholars and mentors during this period, who offered profound guidance that developed a strong sense of social responsibility in the pursuit of scholarship.

By engaging with colleagues of the highest calibre, Goffman built lasting academic connections that would influence his subsequent scholarly partnerships and conversations. His years at the University of Chicago were formative in that he learnt the craft and developed an appreciation for the advances of the discipline. In the stimulating intellectual environment of the University of Chicago, Goffman attained the status of a learnt man, possessing the theory and tools necessary for the construction of his truly exceptional works in the domain of sociology.

Influential Mentors and Colleagues

During his time at the University of Chicago, invaluable mentors and synergistic colleagues illuminated his path with passion and offered unwavering support. Within the context of this academic setting, Erving Goffman, for example, relished the opportunity to interact with leading scholars who played a major role in moulding his sociological imagination. The mentorship of Everett C. Hughes and Herbert Blumer significantly contributed to deepening Goffman's understanding of a wide range of issues. His enriching dialogues with these figures, in turn, provided Goffman with the theoretical tools necessary for an academic culture marked by patent rigour and methodological sophistication. In addition, Goffman's scholarship was also enhanced by the collegial atmosphere of the Chicago scholarly community. The stimulating intellectual context and the enthusiastic exchange of ideas were conducive to the generation of new concepts and the renewal of existing ones. Interaction with those who shared interests in social fieldwork helped Goffman to hone and situate his sociological ideas within new frameworks for further study. The participation of this broad intellectual community, moreover, provided Goffman with the necessary tools that encouraged greater reflexivity, constructive criticism, and an atmosphere of shared progress. The impact of these mentors and colleagues shaped the academic approaches and behavioural claims Goffman made in later papers, essays, and books.

The guidance provided and cooperative relationships developed during this early stage set the stage for an academic career defined by keen observation and critical analysis as well as subtle understanding of the complexities of social conduct. This stage in Goffman's life illustrates the critical importance of guidance and peer interaction in the cultivation of a mental environment conducive to the growth of advanced sociological concepts.

First Forays into Research

Supported by a strong academic background alongside important mentors and colleagues, his first pieces of research were done at the University of Chicago under the supervision of William Thomas. Drawing from his intellectual hunger and formative experiences, he proposed different sociological interrogations and pursued a number of them. One of his earliest research projects looked into the phenomenon of social interactions in metropolitan life, more specifically, the consequences of social structures and social expectations on an individual. Goffman's pioneering work provided fundamental insights into the microstructures of social systems and the interrelations of social properties. Widening the scope of his research, Goffman also studied the process of and the consequences of being stigmatised, and more importantly, the social periphery for the ramifications of that process. It was very different from other sociological studies in his time, as it strove to gain an understanding of the complexities of social systems surrounding social life. Goffman's approach to these micro phenomena was and still is unique. It was this very uniqueness that characterised the complexities of social life. Goffman's work was very meticulous in its research and possessed the empathy of a social observer. For the first time, he revealed the intricate interactions of social life, previously unexplored by sociological discourse. Goffman's earliest exercises in research attested to his sharp mind and his constant intention to reveal the conccaled parts of social interactions and societal frameworks.

Yes, the first foray is micro. It was as a result of social systems. Personal life revolves around an individual's behaviour in a social context. With each of these pursuits, Goffman carved out his own epistemic territory, shifting the focus of sociological imagination to the tiny, often overlooked gestures that carry significant meaning in social interaction. As he travelled to 'the other side' of the world with his works, somehow Goffman had to construct 'the great wall of Goffman' in order to protect his imagination and mental construction and reach that 'new promised land'. Those walls of separation that are the Goffman-Goise balance are not the walls of a fort but the walls of the 'great fortress of Goffman' that was built to protect the Goffman imagination and construction from the jeers of the untented mind. Goffman completed his wall, but only after he was 'torched' on the 'barricades of science' and 'advanced with position'. He last noted the 'science of interactions' on the walls. Goffman marched to prove the Goffman legacy. From that time onwards, and in whatever position he might be in, Goffman was the 'science of structural interactions on Goffman'. Goffman articulated his perspective of the world, placing himself at its centre. Then for a long time, he was the one who constructed that fort on that wall.

Formative Experiences and Challenges

Goffman pursued deeper lines of sociological inquiry and, in the process, went through a number of distinctive experiences and challenges that would shape his later work. Through his self-immersion in the vast urban areas of Chicago, he sought to unravel the sociological complexities and diverse social behavioural patterns. This experience of Goffman reflects his defining moment in the process of this thinking and how he learnt the best way of carrying out a social interaction from a wide range of social contacts. His self-learnt attention and mentally sharpened skills, which were shaped from this experience, built the bedrock of self-theory and the theory of having intersubjective relations. Goffman faced a number of hardships of his own in a growing academic career, and the opposition towards Goffman and his unconventional outlook, as well as the denial of him from certain corners of the discipline, caused a certain sociological scepticism. All these difficulties, while he attempted to manage his academic life effectively, became a source of inspiration rather than a burden and fostered a determined mindset for transforming sociological ideas. From this indicated period in his life, Goffman gathered the most and served as twigs to his interest in having more sociological enquiries, which died out, considering the people who, in turn, became the basis of the sociological documents he was to create.

In addition, Goffman's foray into the social structures within the margins and boundaries of society, while hyperbolic, dealt with the social realities of the underclass, which, in turn, offered him important clues to the problems of stigma and identity. This part of his career, like the others, proves his stamina and courage, calculating that these traits would define his academic journey as he would fight for the advancement of knowledge, regardless of the defeatist intellectual view of the epoch. These tasks or battles permitted Goffman to sharpen his contribution to modern social theory as well as enhance his social conscience. Therefore, the experiences and challenges Goffman encountered in the early stages of his working career shaped his scholarly contributions and commitment in the attempt to uncover the facets of social life.

Laying the Groundwork for Future Theories

At this critical point in Goffman's academic life, he focused on laying the groundwork for new ideas that would transform the field of sociology. As he reflects on his past, meeting challenges head-on, Goffman dedicated his efforts to an intentional, painstaking, and rigorous process of theory construction. Central to his work was an understanding of human social behaviour in social interactions in different contexts. Goffman quickly recognised the potential of these social practices as a wealth of information that could establish the foundations of social order. Goffman's theories were based on the premise that achieving objectives necessitated a deep understanding of the field, passionate observation, and ethnographic research. His rigorous analysis of the "banal" aspects of life in different social contexts yielded him a plethora of raw information of unparalleled depth, which he painstakingly analysed to find social conduct patterns, norms, and hidden structures that govern everyday life. Taking snapshots of the social world, he focused on the micro-level events of people's meetings, pinpointing elements of discourse, motor activity, and signs as social actions, and demonstrating the real consequences of these actions. In addition to that, there was considerable effort on Goffman's part to integrate sociological theories with other disciplines.

With great enthusiasm, he attempted to shift the traditional boundaries of philosophy by integrating psychology, anthropology, and communication into his developing theories. The cross-disciplinary connection further broadened the scope of his research and offered an in-depth insight into how complex human relations and social interactions truly are. Another hallmark of Goffman's foundational work is the continuous elaboration and refinement of his conceptual framework. It is through an iterative process of theorising and refinement that he purged complex observations and empirical data into rational, theoretical frameworks. These scaffolds attempt to explain the outcome of his empirical investigation, which is the social order, identity performance, rituals, and order behaviours, and in return, the verities behind them. In conclusion, Goffman's unyielding undertakings at this stage offered the underpinning that would advance Goffmanian sociology into new territories. The cross-disciplinary, theoretical, and empirical investigation undertaken by Goffman has prepared the sociology field for major conceptual shifts that would alter the course of social science and still be relevant today.

***

Goffman, E. (1989). *On Fieldwork.* Edited by L. H. Waks. *Journal of Contemporary Ethnography*, 18(2), 123–131.

Though brief, this posthumously published note includes rare autobiographical remarks about his early field experiences and intellectual motivations.

1. **Winkin, Y. (2004).** *Erving Goffman: An Intellectual Biography.* In C. Lemert & A. Branaman (Eds.), *The Goffman Reader* (pp. 31–60). Wiley-Blackwell.

This is the most comprehensive biographical account currently available. Winkin traces Goffman's Canadian roots, his undergraduate years in Winnipeg, and his pivotal move to Chicago, showing how his outsider status shaped his observational stance.

2. **Burns, T. (1992).** *Erving Goffman.* Routledge.

Chapter 1 ("The Outsider") situates Goffman's early life in rural Alberta and his Jewish immigrant background as formative to his later focus on stigma, performance, and social marginality. Burns also details his Chicago years and intellectual debts.

3. **Fine, G. A., & Manning, P. K. (2003).** *Erving Goffman.* In G. Ritzer (Ed.), *The Blackwell Companion to Major Social Theorists* (pp. 473–502). Blackwell.

Includes a concise but insightful section on Goffman's education, noting how the **Chicago School's emphasis on urban ethnography and symbolic interactionism** provided the methodological soil for his micro-sociology—even as he diverged from its norms.

4. **Smith, G. W. H. (2006).** *Erving Goffman: A Life in the Interaction Order.* In G. W. H. Smith & A. R. Smith (Eds.), *Erving Goffman* (pp. 1–30). Ashgate.

Focuses on how Goffman's early fieldwork—especially at St Elizabeth's—was rooted in the Chicago tradition of **participant observation**, yet transformed it into a more detached, dramaturgical analysis.

5. **Dromi, S. M., & Fazio, M. (2021).** *"The Iron Cage Revisited": Erving Goffman and the Sociological Canon.* The American Sociologist, 52(4), 605–626. https://doi.org/10.1007/s12108-021-09500-3

While focused on Goffman's legacy, this article includes archival insights into his graduate training at Chicago and his complex relationship with the department's leading figures, particularly Everett Hughes.

6. **Verhoeven, J. C. (1993).** *The Development of Goffman's Ideas: A Critical Appraisal.* In D. Helm, T. J. Anderson, & A. J. Meehan (Eds.), *The Interactional Order: New Directions in the Study of Social Order* (pp. 17–37). Irvington Publishers.

Traces the evolution of Goffman's thought from his Chicago years, showing how he absorbed the school's focus on **urban ecology and selfhood** but rejected its more optimistic view of social integration.

7. **Lemert, C. (2004).** *Why Goffman Is Not a Postmodernist (and Why That Matters).* In C. Lemert & A. Branaman (Eds.), *The Goffman Reader* (pp. 1–28). Wiley-Blackwell.

Contextualises Goffman's early work within postwar American sociology, noting how his Canadian background and Chicago training positioned him as both insider and outsider to U.S. academic culture.

8. **University of Chicago Archives & Special Collections.** See: https://www.lib.uchicago.edu/e/scrc/

Notable item: Goffman's 1953 Ph.D. dissertation, *Communication Conduct in an Island Community* (based on fieldwork in the Shetland Islands), which prefigures *The Presentation of Self*.

Primary archival materials, including departmental records, course catalogues, and correspondence (e.g., letters between Goffman and Everett Hughes), are held at the **University of Chicago Library**. Scholars such as Winkin and Fine have relied on these unpublished materials to ensure biographical accuracy.

2
Finding His Voice
The Shetland Islands and Beyond

Sociological Perspective Emergence

Undoubtedly, one of the most influential sociologists of the 20th century, Erving Goffman constructed the scaffolding for his sociological imagination based on his profound life experiences and the resulting intellectual development. Goffman was born in 1922 in Mannville, Alberta, which, for his age, was an area of cutting-edge socio-cultural innovation, and it was in this context that he began his pioneering investigations of human behaviour. An important formative experience in his life was his early relationship with the culture and society of the Shetland Islands, located off the Scottish coast. This Goffman adopted, immersed in the complex life of the island society, which sculpted his imagination and framework and inspired a serious intellectual inquiry into the sociology of social relations and social identity. The impact of this experience comes out clearly in his influential book The Presentation of Self in Everyday Life, in which he explains the sociological art of 'theatre' in 'everyday life' to elucidate the centrality of performance in human action. This moment in particular helped sharpen Goffman's ability to analyse social behaviour phenomenologically. This context clearly shaped and blossomed Goffman's sociological ideas.

His participation in both rural and urban ecosystems helped him develop a keen understanding of the interdependence between people and their actions and societal systems. By examining the origins of Goffman's sociological ethos, we can establish the foundation of his enduring understanding of human behaviour and social structures, as well as the reasons for his significant contributions to understanding the dynamics of mundane and everyday activities.

Contextual Backdrop: The Shetland Islands Experience

Unlike many worked-over pieces of land, the Shetland Islands lie at the meeting point of the North Atlantic and the North Sea and have since much earlier times captivated both scholars and voyagers by their sheer uniqueness in culture and landform. For the sociologist's pioneering pre-graduate fieldwork, these islands were expendable as the terrain in which the fundamental elements of humanity and the systems which interrelate them were first gleaned. The wild scenery, along with the Shetlanders' age-old neighbour, the sea, and the tales of the islands themselves, formed a concentrated and mind-meditating environment of a unified action where social relationships and bonds were deeply rooted in social behaviour for study and folklore.

The researcher's aspiration to understand the human mind and behaviour within the socio-cultural framework of the society was perfectly matched by the island's isolation and breathtaking beauty. Understanding and living with the islanders made the researcher appreciate the complexities of social life. It also enhanced ethnographic sensibilities, which developed and changed in later pursuits. These remote islands were filled with the everyday life tapestries rich in taken-for-granted rules and unspoken social contracts. These were the building blocks for the formulation of theories that made an enduring contribution to sociology. The pristine and remote sections of the Shetlands nurtured an appreciation for the details of social order and social interrelations. The influence of the Shetlands continues to affect today's social order and interrelations. These blank slates of life in the Shetlands were the motivating factors for inquiry, changing human agency and life in cooperation. These blank slates gave life to an appreciation for the connection between people and the environment.

These blank slates marked the initial stages of fieldwork

The first steps toward fieldwork were the most critical in the history of sociology. Leaving the protective walls of the world of textbooks and the world of the field was the beginning of the major change from synthesis work to immersion.

Goffman's understanding of social life, particularly his fieldwork and accounts of social life, has always, mercifully, departed dramatically from the traditional, nay, orthodox furniture-philosophy style of theorising from an armchair. There was, so to speak, an inner and an outer life. The conclusion is indubitable: every sociologist now has to be seen as a personal participant observer of the intricate social weavings of tapestries. Silence and social 'settings', cognition and culture, demand, one after the other, explanation.

The discovery triggered a rush, a desperation to understand. explored, among other things, in the first place, the individual fieldworker's experience of dealing with so-called remote communities. 'Crucible' is a simple concept. In addition to these people and other worlds as other worlds, the concept of 'acclimatisation' is also used of a world's 'past' geography. This richer culture of empathy is spanned by the resonance of idea empires – an idea is an exosomatic 'cross-pollination', the fertilisation rite of an idea. F Clouds in the milky haze of orbited, seamed worlds – the life-world – in submerged bluish volumes brimming with consciousness also emerged from the work of these indigenous systems of social relations; performed, crafted personal toys and intricate phi-doll networks; and intricate controls of the self and gregariousness. This is where, in social relationships, the more advanced idea – free play, free. In the self-contained transplantation of lineages, of lineages, of enclaves, the other 'worlds' reside. This set a new line of intersecting milky, vortex-born 'swirling', where the observer and the other line. The cocoons' empathy, rhizomatic and weave-connected, between the vanishing worlds, one to two, two to. Each in this pattern serves as an anchor of swirling. Each of these was a new age of 'reflecting' on effect, scanning the experiences gained emerging from these systems as modifications.

Witnessing the performers of everyday life required interpretation and ethical consideration of the dignity of people. Each piece of fieldwork ignited a new curiosity, acquiring manners of social interaction and slowly illuminating the ways people connect to the intricately woven social tapestry. The desire for value and integrity in field narratives serves as a reminder of a sociologist's responsibility to be a guardian of human stories, valuing and protecting them for the purpose of sociological writings. They still stand against the violence and conflict of discursive formation.

Social Interaction Observation in Remote Areas

The first step is still meandering in the field and rushing in the direction of social interaction within remote or secluded areas. Here I was exposed to a rather isolated community. The aim for this particular site was to observe the community's dynamics to better understand how new geographical factors influence social behaviour, interaction, and bonding. Carrying these objectives as an observer of this community demanded immense stretching in imagination about the conditions people live in. The observation of social interactions in these remote locations was rather harmonious and orderly. It was clear to me that geographical distance fosters a relatively new type of social behaviour and interaction.

Other than game theory defining 'connectance', relations between social actors... It observes how reliant we are upon each other for daily physical surroundings, creating intricate social networks of interdependence and constructive, even isolated, social interactions. It reveals within those social networks that gathering institutions and regions form, renew, and set engaging covenants. These relations reinforced crucial structural integration for isolation settlements. Simultaneously, remote actors' disengagement and more intensive scrutiny dynamics crystallised across diverse remote surroundings. Sizeable actor communities permitted actors more awareness and responsiveness, distinguished broader social systems, and extrapolated interaction styles and confirmation. Emphasised remote geography and more interaction with civilisation as primary modes of behaviour. Besides remote chunks, structure dynamics were explored.

Engaging elements of geography and remote social interaction rose sharply. Operation elements derived. Streamlining complexity reaches module research on remote interaction settlements in context. Moreover, building trust and rapport with the community members was essential to obtaining information about the people's social interactions. In the end, studying social interactions in remote areas offered a rich and profound perspective on the impact of geographic isolation on behaviour and relationships. It provided a basis for in-depth consideration of the relationship between distance and social interaction, and prepared for further understanding of the complexity of interactions in different settings.

Influence of Rural Isolation on Methodological Approaches

Conducting sociological research in remote, isolated locations, like the Shetland Islands, influences the conceptualisation of methodological approaches. The social and physical conditions of rural isolation require a flexible and targeted approach. Methodological approaches in such settings must take into account the delicate relationship between people, society, and their defined geospatial environments. Rural isolation fosters specific models of social interaction and community behaviour, which influence the formulation and execution of sociological research methods. The remote, geographic, and populated space, the understanding of which is based on social life in sociological terms, lacks variety, which means approaches cannot be indiscriminately generalised.

Considering these issues makes it imperative to rethink sustainability in methodological frameworks in the contexts of social structure and social agency; rethinking how rural marginality impacts approaches to social research goes well beyond the logistical issues of data retrieval. I argue the chosen research in such settings stimulates the capacity to grasp the finer details of culture to contextualise its penetration of the social fabric. It also compels the researcher to engage in identifying the taken-for-granted biases and assumptions when research is done on physically isolated societies. Also central to the sociological imagination about rural marginality is the concept of 'methodological proximity'. People in such regions being highly interdependent, there is an imperative to reflect on an active interface on which the research subjects relate to the living peculiarities of the phenomena. This is in stark contrast to the traditional settings of research wherein the observer distanced themselves and highlighted the difference between the research to be done and the daily lives of the people, which is the subject of research. This approach intends to reaffirm the close association between the set of social relations and the set of methodological relations and practices and to deepen the set of relations between the researcher and the researched. Methodological approaches to the issue of rural isolation also articulate the necessity to incorporate relations of social phenomena to the variable of time and the contours of social change.

The study of sociology in rural locations calls for an understanding of the timing and history that shapes the community and the longitudinal and diachronic social processes that unfold through time. Furthermore, the impact of rural seclusion on research techniques illustrates the need for reflexivity and considerable 'multisensory' awareness of the social ecologies of distant and secluded contexts.

Cultural Adaptation and Learning

Completing sociological research on the Shetland Islands, and the need to adapt to different cultures, is crucial to the research. This understanding, which involves shifting from one culture to another and integrating oneself, is essential for grasping the nuances of that culture. This understanding makes the process of integrating oneself easier. It is how Goffman treated his time on the Shetland Islands. Learning a culture and its practices is slow. Fully immersing oneself in the culture involves being active in the community and understanding both the people and their practices. This is what Goffman focused on in his understanding. He concentrated on what the social structure is, what the phenomenon behind the social structure is, and the deep social structure within the community. Learning is continuous, and culture is another form of civilised life. Every contact is a teaching, and observing is a learning. It requires thinking differently and considering oneself and the outside.

Goffman's ability to adapt and learn from the inhabitants of the Shetland Islands enriched his sociological imagination about human behaviour. Furthermore, the ability to adapt to the new culture and society involves engaging with ethical issues surrounding the faithful representation of the community's narratives and belief systems. Goffman understood the consequences his presence may have on the community's social structure, especially how his notes and conclusions would shape how the outside world would come to see the island community. This form of self-reflection, or self-separation, drove Goffman as he experienced it on the island and contemplated the consequences of his work, which he was keen to make responsible. Ultimately, the ability to navigate a new culture and society, alongside learning, are two very vital steps in the development of sociological methods. Goffman, while traversing the Shetland Islands and deeply analysing its social relations, improved his ability to notice and think about the world around him, developed new methods of thinking, and gained a new appreciation for the complexities of the simple practices of life. These elements formed the very foundation of the unique aspects of his future research work, which in turn laid the groundwork for the new boundaries he established within the discipline of sociology.

Development of Analytical Techniques

As part of his fieldwork, Goffman had to create new social settings. In this instance, he needed to develop methods of human interaction.

This undertaking represented a defining moment in his academic career, as it involved a rather complex fusion of intricate methodological processes and an ability to shift to different cultural environments. Goffman appreciated the necessity of divergent thinking beyond the confines of classical sociological thought to deeply penetrate the realities of social interaction. He transformed into a full-fledged sociologist, embracing elements from psychology, anthropology, and communication, and striving to integrate various streams of thought into a single analytical framework. Goffman was also at the forefront of advanced social thinking in articulating ideas that captured the essence of social behaviour. Through careful recording and keen observation, he captured the dynamics of social life and the patterns that characterised the ways people dressed and adorned themselves for different social contexts. He suggested the phrase 'impression management' as one of the foundational concepts of his theory: to account for the processes people undergo, both consciously and unconsciously, to control the way others perceive them. He also coined the term 'dramaturgical analysis' to describe his interpretation of social relations as a performance in which every participant assumes and acts out different roles on a social stage according to the social rules of the interaction. Goffman also grappled with the development of systematic observational methods that would record the subtleties of normal social encounters.

His dedication to improving new techniques resulted in participant observation, unobtrusive observation, and other field note techniques. These acquired methods allowed Goffman to go beyond traditional survey methods. He went further and used social life in its organic form to attain a deeper understanding of social behaviour. As Goffman walked through and within a maze of different social setups, he polished and added new words to his growing vocabulary. He introduced fundamental terms like "face-saving behaviour," "interaction rituals," and "the presentation of oneself." Every term was the result of thorough research and detail, showing Goffman's resolve to understand the subtleties of social actions. These skills in analysis ultimately changed the course of symbolic interactionism and confirmed Goffman's place in sociology.

Challenges and Discoveries: Exploring Unfamiliar Territories

In crossing the Shetland Islands, the sociologist faced a multitude of challenges and intriguing insights. New territories posed a set of obstacles that stretched his methods and sociocultural flexibility.

The challenge was to learn and assimilate into various unfamiliar sociocultural environments. It was no longer as simple as grasping the interwoven island life. The city offered intricate societal frameworks. The study exposed the intricate layers of interaction that the previously individualistic islander had become accustomed to. The overt sense of individualisation was a stark contrast to the hectic lifestyle of the city. There was interwoven anonymity and mastery of multiple intricate urban systems. There was mastery over public postures, spacing, and individualistic and collective dispositions in urban areas. The social systems were reduced and covered. While grappling with and navigating novel territories, individuals found that the functioning of outer structures created working subcultures and distinct behavioural codes. These complex subcultures and sociological structures provided inner territories needing fresh restructuring. Multiple social groups were expressed. The diverse urban subcultures in which people live and work can be best described as existing within a specific context. Multiple urban domains within which people live and work could best be described as urban patchworks. The study of context enables an understanding of the behavioural aspects, clarifying the context of the inquiry. It touches the essence of the urban order, devoid of boundaries which segregate the social fabric.

Despite these challenges, he also made captivating discoveries that enhanced those pursuits. His entry into various contexts highlighted the extraordinarily diverse range of relationships and interactions and the complex ways in which societies adapt and diversify. The sociologist managed to describe a wide range of social phenomena, such as urban non-verbal communication and new forms of collective identity emerging in the city. All in all, the sociologist's ability to adapt to new terrains seems to have facilitated a deeper understanding of the fascinating social phenomena as well as the ability to conquer new challenges.

Recognising Daily Interaction Patterns

Finding patterns in how people interact with each other every day is an important goal for understanding how society works and how people act. Figuring out these complicated patterns shows how social life is structured. This is based on smart observations and experiences gained from moving through different environments. Here, we discuss the careful steps that go into finding and studying these kinds of behaviour patterns. We also talk about how important they are for research in sociology.

The core of this investigation lies in the intense immersion in diverse social contexts, allowing the researcher to identify the nuances of interpersonal dynamics. By fully engaging with the daily routines of communities, one can grasp the repetitive gestures, rituals, and expressions that define social behaviour. Through careful observation and sharp insight, the small but important differences in gestures, verbal cues, and non-verbal communication are made clear, showing how complicated human interaction can be.

The interpretation of these observed patterns is bolstered by systematic methodologies rooted in empirical rigour. The comprehensive data gathered, encompassing meticulous note-taking and audio-visual documentation, constructs an intricate representation of social behaviours. These carefully recorded observations serve as the foundation for comprehensive analysis, aiming to identify underlying structures and recurring themes within all interactions.

Through qualitative and quantitative analytical frameworks, the differentiation between individual agency and societal norms is clarified, yielding substantial insights into the interplay between micro-level interactions and macro-level societal constructs.

Furthermore, the dynamic nature of these identified patterns requires an exhaustive analysis of contextual elements and temporal fluctuations. When we look closer, we can see the social, cultural, historical, and environmental factors that are part of these patterns. This illustrates the continual evolution and adaptation of social dynamics. Therefore, a comprehensive understanding of everyday interactions necessitates an interdisciplinary approach, amalgamating sociological, anthropological, and psychological perspectives to thoroughly capture the intricate aspects of human behaviour.

Ultimately, discerning patterns in daily human interactions enhances academic discourse and significantly influences real-world dynamics. The clarification of these subtle yet significant behavioural patterns improves our comprehension of the intricate structure of human society, laying the groundwork for future scholarly investigation and societal progress."

Conclusion: Supporting the groundwork for scholarly engagement

Placing this inquiry into the primary formative influences for the sociological thinking of Goffman, what comes to light in the very first place is the impact of the Shetland Islands and their beyond. Placement beyond urban context proves to provide the setting relevant for Goffman at a very early stage to understand in the first instance the elementary and base social behaviour relevant in all parts of the world. Goffman's sociological thinking extends well beyond the boundaries of the Shetland Islands.

His devotion to grasping the subtle distinctions that characterise daily life activities resolutely combined with the performances that environment executes on the frameworks of societal systems truly opened gateways for other scholars to contemplate the more complex aspects of human relationship systems. One of the emblematic outcomes derived from Goffman's stay in the Shetland Islands pertains to the formulation of refined methods of analysis based on the systematic study of the social order and behavioural patterns.

Goffman's Osmond and the probes he made on the micro

level of the social structure unlocked more of Goffman's work on the social structure and order, and the aspects that control the people were more of the lionisation. This has also become a foundational work for scholars interested in further studying society.

Goffman, instead, went on to particular techniques and mastered the difficult techniques on isolation, especially in these specific cases. These techniques would reveal the depth of the phenomena and illustrate the cultural context.

Today, Goffman's work inspires a growing number of scholars to employ interdisciplinary and fieldwork approaches, which are more fulfilling methods closely linked to sociological fieldwork.

Finding new insights in Goffman's work has always been of importance and gives direction towards new enquiries, which showcases the importance of the groundwork of Goffman's work in the comprehension of the subtleties of social relations. Whether Goffman's younger days shaped his influence in the world of sociology is a question too far explored. It is not to be questioned that the observations made, and the methods employed during that time, became primary resources for the sociological scholars who came after him. The time spent in the Shetland Islands during his childhood is a prime example of the positivity that comes from proper fieldwork, culture, and the expenditure of analysis. It is easy to say Goffman's work has and will be a great influence for the coming years for people studying the relations and sociology of people.

***

Primary source:
Goffman, E. (1989). *On Fieldwork*. Edited by L. H. Waks. Journal of Contemporary Ethnography, 18(2), 123–131.

A rare, posthumously published reflection where Goffman discusses his observational stance, noting, "*I have always been more interested in the stage than the backstage... in what is publicly available to the eye.*"

1. **Rawls, A. W. (2000).** "*The Interaction Order*" (1983) and the "*Interaction Order*" (2000): *Goffman's Legacy for Sociology*. American Sociological Review, 65(5), 741–749. https://doi.org/10.2307/2657543

Rawls argues that Goffman's focus on the interaction order represents a **radical alternative epistemology**—one that grounds social theory in observable, situated practices rather than abstract structures. She shows how this demands a rethinking of what counts as "data" in sociology.

2. **Emerson, R. M. (2011).** "*On Goffman: Fieldwork, Observation, and the Interaction Order.*" In R. M. Emerson, R. I. Fretz, & L. L. Shaw (Eds.), *Writing Ethnographic Fieldnotes* (2nd ed., pp. 25–48). University of Chicago Press.

Demonstrates how Goffman's observational sensibility—his attention to posture, glance, timing, and spatial arrangement—profoundly shaped modern ethnographic practice, even though he rarely labelled his work "ethnography".

3. **Winkin, Y. (1988).** *Erving Goffman: An Intellectual Biog-*

raphy. University of California Press.

Traces how Goffman's method emerged from his rejection of grand theory. Winkin shows that Goffman saw the sociologist not as a detached theorist but as a **"collector of social facts"**—a meticulous observer of the "furniture" of everyday life (queues, greetings, glances).

4. **Manning, P. K. (1992).** *Erving Goffman and Modern Sociology*. Stanford University Press.

Chapter 2 ("The Sociologist as Observer") analyses Goffman's unique stance: neither fully participant nor fully detached, but a **"moral witness"** to the fragility of social order. Manning emphasises Goffman's literary style as a methodological choice—eschewing jargon to preserve the texture of lived experience.

5. **Burns, T. (1992).** *Erving Goffman*. Routledge.

Burns highlights Goffman's debt to **phenomenology (Schutz) and ethnomethodology (Garfinkel)**, both of which reject armchair philosophy in favour of studying how people *actually* make sense of their world. Goffman, Burns argues, turned sociology into a **"poetics of the ordinary".**

6. **Goode, J. (2020).** *Goffman's Method: The Art of Sociological Observation*. Symbolic Interaction, 43(4), 553–574. https://doi.org/10.1002/symb.490

A recent reassessment that frames Goffman not as a theorist who occasionally observed, but as an **observer who theorised through description**. Goode shows how Goffman's "data" were the **micro-details of conduct**—silences, hesitations, body angles—that traditional sociology ignored.

7. **Fine, G. A. (2001).** "The Curious Case of Erving Goffman: His Context and Our Canon." In G. A. Fine, *Gifted Tongues: High School Debate and Adolescent Culture* (pp. 215–236). Princeton University Press.

Fine reflects on how Goffman's **anti-systematic style**—his use of vignettes, irony, and marginal examples—was both his genius and the reason he was never fully "canonised" in orthodox theory courses, despite his ubiquity.

8. **Atkinson, P. (2015).** *For Ethnography.* Sage Publications.

Though not solely about Goffman, Atkinson positions him as a **proto-ethnographer of the mundane**. He argues that Goffman's work exemplifies what ethnography should be: attentive to **settings, embodiment, and the "silent syntax" of social life**—precisely the "intricate social weavings" your passage evokes.

3
The Scholar as Outsider
A Complex Relationship With the Discipline

Introduction to Goffman's Outsider Status

Goffman had an academic outsider status, which affected his innovative sociological work. Every scholar faces academic problems, which often stem from their outsider status. Goffman's beginnings in Canada and the lack of an elite pedigree in his graduate education due to inflated sociological documents from his days at Chicago University pose an 'othered' gaze, which might be beneficial in the theory of social behaviours. The academic challenges Goffman had to face originated from his peculiar theory of constructing sociological documents. He strayed from the canon norms and was therefore in opposition to the "received" knowledge. Goffman, by nature, balances his theoretical and methodological stances with gaps to work. He invests in Goffman's sociological imagination. Goffman's already non-conformist outsider status was forged in great part by the cross-disciplinary frames he was drawing from. These universal constructs were used to marry social theory with anthro-sociological frames, plus psychology and the discipline of communication, to create something pertaining to Goffman's ecology, which enriches the analysis of the Web.

Erving Goffman's **outsider status in academia**—despite his immense influence—is a well-documented and often-discussed theme in sociological literature. Though widely read and cited, Goffman was frequently viewed as **marginal to mainstream sociological theory**, partly due to his:

- Preference for **micro-level analysis** over grand

theory

- Use of **literary, ironic, and anecdotal styles** rather than formal academic prose

- Avoidance of explicit **methodological declarations** or data tables

- Scepticism toward **structural-functionalism, Marxism, and positivism** dominant in mid-20th-century sociology

- Position as a **Canadian Jewish intellectual** in elite American institutions (University of Chicago, UC Berkeley, University of Pennsylvania)

Scholars have interpreted this "outsider" position both as a **limitation** (e.g., lack of theoretical systematization) and a **strength** (e.g., freedom to innovate, critique norms from the margins).

Furthermore, Goffman himself acknowledged his marginality. In his 1982 ASA presidential address ("The Interaction Order"), he noted that his work had been "treated as if it were not quite sociology"—a quiet lament that underscores his complex relationship with the discipline.

Early Academic Challenges

The relationship of Goffman with academia was marked by the tension of his alien status and the expectations of the institution concerning scholarly interaction. Goffman was able to maintain his freedom and did not conform to the expectations of the status quo, as much as he was confronted, and settled on a particular niche for himself within the academic world. Being an 'outsider' in the role of 'fieldworker' helped him garner much deeper insights into the subtle attributes of social life. He was able to develop some of his most critical concepts and theories because of this.

The influence Goffman's outsider point of view brought to sociological theorising was and continues to be tremendous. With the sociological imagination, Goffman was able to breach the walls of some traditional academic imagery; Goffman was able to broaden the scope of social interaction and the formation of self.

The sociological Goffman was more than willing to protect the bones of his sisters and brothers, and in doing this he also had to take the heat of criticism, disputes, and the dreads of orthodoxy defence. The innovation of Goffman's approach was and will always be in conflict with the mainstream sociological apprehension because of the tension which will always exist in sociological boundaries.

As an outsider, Goffman did not only assist sociology with theories; he also inspired new generations of sociologists to look at the field in a new light filled with unconventional ideas and multidisciplinary approaches.

The impact Goffman continues to have today has evoked the most critical self-evaluation, especially concerning the role of 'outsiders' in academic work and what they refer to as 'alternative' viewpoints.

Interdisciplinary Influences and Intellectual Independence

Many connections and frustrations confronted him in the early stages of his life as an academic that he had to overcome to be able to fulfil his dreams as a scholar.

While still a scholar in training, Goffman, due to what some called 'unique' characteristics of his research interests and teasing methodologies, faced resistance and scepticism from some circles of academia. The very nature of Goffman's interests in studying stigmatised social phenomena and his propensity to undertake 'unorthodox' research methodologies were sources of conflict between him and the dominant frameworks in most academic disciplines. Hard as it was to imagine, Goffman, even with his intellectual gifts, faced institutional hurdles of discrimination and prejudice in his first years of academic work. The very essence of the new ideas he developed and the conceptions he was willing to entertain were so foreign to the dominant approaches that they made it necessary for him to move in a world that, according to most, was simply 'untoward' and 'unusual' for what he was doing. Moreover, the unorthodox nature of studying the groups that were labelled as 'deviant' was the source of disdain and scepticism from the rest of academia. Goffman made academic 'niches' for himself with great difficulty for what everyone considered 'academic' scepticism and adversity. This, in turn, probably made Goffman the most 'influenced' in how and what he did sociologically. Working under these conditions, he 'had to', as sociologists put it, move against the grain of what was acceptable, and it was unique in its own way – freedom of how he worked.

Innovative Methodologies and Unconventional Approaches

Goffman's scholarly work shows he had the ability to design new techniques that would illuminate phenomena that other workers overlooked. His pioneering work in participant observation was the first to use this technique to immerse himself in different social settings. This participation was necessary to understand the firsthand context of what people do in their daily routines. This technique facilitated the grasping of subtle aspects of social behaviour that would otherwise be neglected even by the prominent scholars of the field. Moreover, Goffman borrowed notions from dramaturgy and from the theory of symbolic interactionism to design novel analytic tools intended to analyse social actions. The tools demonstrated in the field were not confined to the existing sociological practices in researching social phenomena. Goffman's use of novel analytic tools for sociological phenomena made him both a celebrated and controversial figure. Apart from this, Goffman's novel analytic tools extended to sociology itself. He did not write in the common sociological style that is laden with jargon and claim-filled sentences; instead, he narrated stories that communicated the main ideas and all the subtle nuanced ideas in a manner that people not in the field could easily grasp. Goffman's use of simple, vivid language made him a recognised figure beyond the sociological community.

Also, the use of storytelling and vivid descriptions added

numerous layers of depth and richness to Goffman's research findings, allowing readers to become engrossed in the social worlds he examined. In combining new and creative methods, Goffman changed the sociology field by adding new elements and leaving a lasting impression on the field that still motivates newer sociologists today.

Interdisciplinary Influences and Intellectual Independence

Diverse interdisciplinary relations and personal freedom in thought were significant factors in the sociological work of Erving Goffman. His work came from several different disciplines, including psychology, anthropology, and communication, as well as symbolic interaction. Goffman's work embraced the exploration of human beings from a truly interdisciplinary perspective. His personal freedom in thought allowed him to go beyond the orthodox constraints of a single discipline, and this motivated him to provide new frameworks, as well as constructs that still impact a myriad of fields today. Goffman's active participation in a whole range of disciplines provided an intricate and sophisticated grasp of social relations, as well as social processes. His work in research was novel, as he demonstrated an undying commitment to originality, and his dedication was the reason he fought against the norms and paradigms. His ability to show a great deal of boldness intellectually made him stand out as a unique scholar whose work was not associated with any particular discipline.

Incorporating different theories and techniques across

disciplines, he expanded the sociological imagination and provided novel ways of thinking about human social life. Especially, Goffman's interdisciplinary divagations were important for moulding the progressive attitude he had toward social phenomena, which resulted in the first of his many contributions to the study of human interactions. His intellectual freedom had the full effect of empowering him to analyse the existing beyond the box, and because of this, paradigm shifting for the evolution of sociology occurred. In addition, Goffman's interdisciplinary thinking from which he worked benefited the relevance of his studies, which made his impact wider than the borders of academia. His intellectual freedom in this case was a sharpened marker of the relevance of taking interdisciplinary fronts in sociological knowledge and theories.

Goffman's Relationship with Academia

The relationship of Erving Goffman to the academe looked like a complex mixture of admiration, doubt and liberty. In his capacity as a prominent sociologist, Goffman was both worshipped and blamed as a result of his creativity and unorthodox methods of conducting research. His controversial character and critical thinking scorned the acceptable rules and standards, making him a bathroom reader of the world.

Goffman's academic journey highlighted the importance of free-standing thoughts poring over the conflicts and debates of the period, which modernised the understanding of social activities and human behaviour. With trying opposition and doubt from the academic world, he committed himself to identifying the delicate details of the self and the social in the daily routine and everyday life. Couched somewhere in the middle of sociology, anthropology and psychology, Goffman took the road less travelled, which interconnected disciplines and drew from all of them to enrich the theorems and methods he proposed. His multiple domain interactions indeed added richness and subtlety to his thoughts but also took them out of the clutch of any single academic parent. Goffman, although rooted in originality and profundity, was simultaneously perceived as distant from the regulatory mechanisms of the academic world. His behaviour of non-compliance as well as disinterest in the so-called 'standard' academic world drew a mixture of sentiments. His reputation was somehow protected as a true maverick because he did the impossible with his commitment to authentically understanding every matter he investigated.

Examining social life along with the performances that construct shared realities has become one of the overarching pillars of puppet-master scholarship; in fact, the artist's legacy has an important place in the global world of academia, instilling motivation for fresh scholars while also fuelling criticism in every contemporary theorist.

Resistance to Normative Expectations

Throughout his scholarly career, Goffman faced no end of challenges from the academic community for his refusal to endorse Goffman's 'hypothetical' approach to sociology. Goffman was, by nature, an original thinker, one who systematically practised individualised sociology, often deconstructing the reigning assumptions of the field. To Goffman, the issue was not in rebellion for the sake of rebellion. To Goffman, the focus was social life as it exists, in all its complexity. Goffman did not fit the mould of an orthodox researcher; Goffman was a thinker who was willing to 'think outside of the box' in order to get beneath the surface of social life. The need to escape from the boundaries of sociology led him to construct other methods of his work, which include, but are not limited to, participant observation and ethnographic work. Goffman's developed methods of research were not exclusively driven by the results of research; his critique was that the 'expectation that a researcher behaves in normatively acceptable ways was far from the mark, as he did not shy away from the controversial'. Deviance and identity are but a few of the sociological concepts that preoccupied him. Above all, Goffman's thoughts and notions were the focus of 'the' sociological analysis. Goffman's illustrations were often considered not in tune with his counterparts. Evidence of this is his hyper-logical writing, which was a departure from the norm.

In addition to those psychological and anthropological insights that he drew on along with literary theories, he showed unwillingness to be boxed within a discipline, choosing a rather broader approach. By overcoming expectations of a rigid approach to sociology, Goffman provided an opportunity for the revitalisation of thinking within the discipline and facilitated the advancement of the social sciences. The legacy teaches him about the defiant nature of the old order and the need to advocate such to produce authentic understandings.

Fieldwork as an Outsider Practice

Fieldwork as an outsider practice remains of paramount importance in the scholarly undertaking to comprehend social actions and the workings of an institution. For Erving Goffman, fieldwork was done on the basis of the author as an outsider, which, in turn, placed him on the periphery of the social order, offering an observation and analytical position from where he could understand social actions. Goffman was able to understand the practice of fieldwork in rather novel ways, to the extent that his outsider status informed as well as motivated him to embrace intricate social interaction relations.

In his fieldwork, Goffman studied a range of settings, including his dealing with the challenges of mental facilities and asylums, where he was able to embody an outsider and, at the same time, used this outsider view as an advantage to strengthen his understanding of the details of social life. His fieldwork as an outsider enabled him to plunge head-on into uncharted waters, thus exposing social stigmas, the exercise of power, and the making of a personal identity in different social contexts. His fieldwork was methodical and with strong inferences as he converted it to a tool for shedding light on social life. His ability to conduct fieldwork was matched with the sociological principle at hand, and the embracing of an outsider view deeply enriched the sociological understanding of the phenomena. Goffman has demonstrated that fieldwork and sociological inquiry on social phenomena would be deeply enriched from a disengaged manner. From a different sociological perspective, Goffman has shown that fieldwork would sample behaviour and norms with an unbounded understanding of life, and the possibility of a disengaged understanding would greatly inform them, such as social engagement ethics that are grounded to bring about changes in behaviour in a wider sociological context.

Impact of Outsider Perspective on Sociological Theory

The outsider perspective from scholars like Erving Goffman has greatly influenced the development of sociological theory.

Completing this assignment has provided scholars with the ability to adopt a creative approach to observing human actions and social behaviour and offer a perspective that differs from the commonly accepted norms. As expected, this perspective will profoundly challenge the established theories and methodologies within the discipline and will necessitate a rethinking of the extensive lines of sociological thought. This capacity to adopt an outsider view is a significant advantage that sociologists utilise to reveal the complexities of social relations that are typically concealed and difficult to articulate. Taking a perspective external to the core of society enables sociologists to perceive the visibility that is hidden from the world, which is the fundamental social routine. The social life viewed as residual, peripheral, and marginal has substantially advanced sociological thinking.

Furthermore, the outsider perspective has been crucial in dismantling the exaggerated generalisations and misconceptions that are often taken for granted. Scholars, as outsiders, have managed to deconstruct the dominant simplifications within social theories, illustrating how the social world is more intricate than it is frequently assumed to be. This questioning of social norms and conventions has opened new avenues for examining social behaviour and interactions in a more nuanced way and has, as a result, nurtured a more sophisticated level of sociological thought.

The inclusion of an outsider perspective within sociological theory aids in promoting interdisciplinary engagement and acts as a catalyst for paradigm shifts. The application of unorthodox methodologies has spurred innovations within the study of human society. Their involvement has encouraged theoretical dialogue and the exchange of ideas both within and outside the disciplines, enriched frameworks, and integrated novel sets of theories.

Additionally, the outsider perspective helps to provide reflexivity and sociological self-awareness in relation to sociological studies. Scholars, by recognising their sociological 'outsiderism', are able to critically analyse their own positions and, in turn, enhance both the rigour and the quality of sociological research. This self-evaluation tends to enrich the academic landscape by pursuing intellectual rigour and facilitating shifts in conversations regarding the impacts of varying perspectives on how knowledge is constructed.

Identifying the contribution of the outsider perspective to sociological theory involves undergoing a process of acknowledging the sociological imagination. It has reflexively fostered interdisciplinary collaboration, broadened the scope of sociological inquiry, strengthened the sociological discipline, and paradoxically challenged the taken-for-granted sociological theories. The sociological imagination is compelling in that it continually inspires sociological scholarship. The effortless simplicity and insight into the intricacies of human social life enrich this scholarship.

Criticisms and Disputes with Mainstream Thought

As is well known, this is particularly true of Erving Goffman, who espoused the form of an 'outsider' perspective in the realm of sociological thought. This status of 'outsider' led, as is also widely acknowledged, to numerous arguments and criticisms directed at Goffman's contributions by leading figures in the field.

One of the most critical areas of dispute stems from Goffman's attention to the micro level of social behaviour and its focus as symbolic social behaviour, an angle that some thinkers argued away from concentrating on structural imbalances and systemic inequality. Critics of Goffman argue that by focusing on interpersonal conduct and communication, he abstracted too much from the overarching social superstructures as well as the domination relations of the social order, and he failed to account for the elementary phenomena in the social order, particularly class, race, and gender. This argument also concerns Goffman's theorising on stigma and labelling, which some people blame for the overly simplified social constructions, while actually, social structures and the predominant values of society largely determine the situation an individual is in. Furthermore, much of Goffman's work on the dramaturgical perspective has been critiqued for its tendency to promote the conservative view that the social world is so organised that all people do is 'manage' social 'impressions' and 'put on' social 'masks' while more fundamental social 'problems' do exist. Additionally, Goffman is most reproached due to the ethnographic method he employed, the extent to which he was able to scientifically document the validity of the conclusions he reached, as well as the subjective and, particularly, the biased issues arising from participant observation.

In addition, outside of contests with the dominant paradigm, there is a focus on the ethical dimensions of Goffman's research, which negatively concern informed consent, the right to privacy, and the possible 'dangers' of revealing sensitive interpersonal relations.

Several critics have raised disputes about Goffman's unconventional techniques, especially regarding ethical issues; since his methods remain unresolved, the ethics of his work continue to attract criticism. However, the criticisms aimed at him also make it plausible to argue that his work continues to evoke discussions that are outside the box and raise the proverbial bar of ethics. He liberalises people's understanding of sociology and the issues surrounding it.

Legacy of Goffman's Outsider Scholarship

Erving Goffman's work still inspires and continues to remain relevant today. Goffman's legacy rests on the interdisciplinary domains of sociology; his work still stands, and his lack of conformity and his willingness to confront the social orthodoxies to investigate social behaviours define Goffman's lifetime achievement. Erving Goffman, an outsider scholar, profoundly shaped and imprinted on the field of sociology, further enriching it. Also, the contrasting facets about Goffman that are most intriguing are that the outsider perspective he offers transcends orthodox sociological theorising the most and that it is Goffman's.

The attention that he pays to the stigmatised and the processes of social exchange in multiple contextualised settings has created a foundation that many other scholars have built upon to analyse identity, power, and social control. In addition, the interdisciplinary impact of Goffman's work is apparent in the enduring legacy he left behind. The integration of his sociology with other disciplines, such as sociology with anthropology, psychology, and the science of communications, created the depth and breadth of his scholarship. The same breadth of approach he took to his work has influenced other scholars in multiple disciplines, deepening the understanding of social phenomena and the behaviours that define and shape them. Outside of the institutional setting, Goffman's work has been applied in the fields of counselling, social work, and even criminal justice. The policies and practices designed by social planners and anti-stigmatisation campaigners have, to a large extent, been informed by the outsider Goffman perspective on practice that seeks to advance social integration and the transformation of social and institutional practices as a means of social justice. It is clear that Goffman's work serves as an inspiration for what scholarship in sociology can do in tackling social problems. His work serves as an example of what effective social action can do. In the remaining part of his work, Goffman's philosophy has shown that the impact of his scholarship has withstood the test of time and surpasses disciplinary confines. The changes he brought in as an outsider have been central to understanding how human beings relate with one another as well as the systems that govern their interactions. Advanced research activities inspire developed and emerging scholars to analyse social life from the outsider's perspective; this includes engaging with silenced voices and transcending the traditional anthropological frameworks.

***

1. **Fine, G. A., & Manning, P. K. (2003).** *Erving Goffman.* In G. Ritzer (Ed.), The Blackwell Companion to Major Social Theorists (pp. 473–502). Blackwell Publishing.

Discusses how Goffman was "never fully embraced by the sociological mainstream" despite his popularity. Highlights tensions between his literary style and disciplinary expectations of rigour.

2. **Burns, T. (1992).** *Erving Goffman.* Routledge.

Chapter 1 ("The Outsider") explicitly frames Goffman as an intellectual outsider—geographically, stylistically, and theoretically. Burns argues that Goffman's marginality enabled his unique perspective on social norms and deviance.

3. **Rawls, A. W. (2002).** *Editor's Introduction: Interaction Order and Social Theory.* In E. Goffman, The Interaction Order (reprinted in *Sociological Theory*, 20(3), 269–302).

Rawls notes that Goffman's focus on the "interaction order" was long dismissed as "merely descriptive" by structural theorists, contributing to his outsider reputation—even as his ideas quietly shaped ethnography, linguistics, and communication studies.

4. **Lemert, C. (2004).** "Why Goffman Is Not a Postmodernist (and Why That Matters)." In C. Lemert & A. Branaman (Eds.), *The Goffman Reader* (pp. 1–28). Wiley-Blackwell.

Lemert reflects on Goffman's uneasy fit within any theoretical camp—neither a symbolic interactionist in the Blumerian sense, nor a postmodernist, nor a critical theorist—making him a "theorist without a home."

5. **Smith, G. W. H. (2006).** *Erving Goffman: Theorising the Self in a World of Appearances.* In G. W. H. Smith & A. R. Smith (Eds.), *Erving Goffman* (pp. 1–30). Ashgate.

Explores how Goffman's refusal to engage with macro-social theory (e.g., class, power, history) led many sociologists to view him as apolitical or superficial—reinforcing his outsider status in critical sociology circles.

6. **Dromi, S. M., & Fazio, M. (2021).** "The Iron Cage Revisited": Erving Goffman and the Sociological Canon. *American Sociologist, 52*(4), 605–626. https://doi.org/10.1007/s12108-021-09500-3

A recent empirical analysis of Goffman's citation patterns and reception in top sociology journals. Shows that while widely cited, he is rarely engaged as a *theorist*—often reduced to a "quotation machine" for concepts like stigma or dramaturgy.

7. **Manning, P. K. (1992).** "Goffman's Irony and the Moral Career of a Sociologist." In *Erving Goffman and Modern Sociology* (pp. 1–25). Stanford University Press.

The author argues that Goffman's ironic tone, avoidance of moralising, and focus on surface behaviour alienated him from sociologists invested in emancipatory or normative projects, portraying him as a detached observer rather than a committed intellectual.

8. **Winkin, Y. (2004).** *Erving Goffman: An Intellectual Biography.* In C. Lemert & A. Branaman (Eds.), *The Goffman Reader* (pp. 31–60). Wiley-Blackwell.

Traces Goffman's biography—from Winnipeg to Berkeley—and shows how his cultural background and personal reserve contributed to his perception as an aloof, enigmatic figure outside academic networks and orthodoxies.

Part II: Major Works and Core Concepts

4
The Dramaturgical Perspective
The Social Stage

A Brief History of Dramaturgical Analysis

Dramaturgical analysis is a powerful new way of looking at social life—with a focus on the social actions of people in the context of their daily activities. In social life, as in theatre, people put on performances. In this chapter, we start from this insight. In terms of performance, each person is like an actor on a stage who scripts and performs different sides of themselves to different people and in different social situations. The use of roles, props, walks, and performances on stage makes the social world richer and more interesting. The added dimension that a social world gains as a result of the participation of an actor is the focus of this analysis. Dramaturgical analysis, in particular, has been used in the social sciences to help make sense of how people actively construct and navigate their social worlds through impression management and presentation of self in everyday life. This is also to help make sense of social actions in their context and the shifting balances of personal agency and structure. Additionally, the tools of social life that answer the question of how reality is constructed and meaning negotiated in different social settings are also explained with the help of dramaturgical analysis.

The scholarly integration of social self-portrayal, audience perception, and non-verbal communication feedback serves to assist researchers in better understanding and answering questions related to social order, identity construction, and the continuous social interchange of cultural scripts. The answer to the questions lies in the use of dramaturgical analysis. The analysis is the answer to the complex social problems posed. It captures the entire experience of a person and allows them to understand the analysis deeply to comprehend the interactions of the individuals in the focal area and the performances conducted in the social theatre of life.

The Social Interaction: Theatre Metaphor

In social interactions, Goffman's perspective is dramatic; the use of the word 'analogy' is metaphorical. There is a close description of how people shift in social life in relation to the performances on the stage. It enables the audience to think of social interactivity and communication as more rehearsed. Similar to a stage where actors take on different roles and play characters, people also take on different roles and masks in order to navigate the complexities of daily life. The social stage is an active stage where people assume different masks and costumes in order to perform and manage their image and portray characters to the audience. The 'Theatrum Mundi' perspective provides Goffman with the insight from which he builds a social 'backstage' area. This is akin to the backstage of a theatre—in the social realm, it is the place where people are no longer expected to perform and are able to act authentically. The backstage portion of social settings provides enormous freedom. The metaphors of the theatre allow us to see more deeply into the way people socialise and the techniques people deploy to develop and sustain their social identity. Also, it directs attention to how much those being perceived, and the audience, do in the interaction. Putting it mildly, it is a sociology, which from about Goffman's time started to be defined and studied, and is a 'theatrical sociology'. Through the prism of dramaturgy, the social nature of interaction systems transcends any and all complexities of the social construction of reality, to which each individual is ever more deeply intertwined. The more we focus on the social interplay of theatre, the more of the prism its sociology loses; to the extent it becomes a complex of new forms of understanding, it is no longer the behaviour in question but the interplay of the roles, the scripts and the stages we interweave in the wide and ever-widening society.

Frontal and Performance Parts

Social behaviour, from the perspective of dramaturgy, is akin to being on stage, where each person has to perform a particular role and, in the process, take a deliberate posture in order to control the image they present to the audience.

From this perspective, life becomes a stage, illuminating how people employ different masks in life and how they engage in life. Masks are the costumes and manners people wear and use in social interactions, which involve their body, gestures, and vocal sounds. Front-stage activities are those driven by social psychology and the constructs that come with a particular social role. A physician, for example, is expected to engage in a particular behaviour which is characterised by a set of standards and a particular warped reality. Professional behaviour, which involves certain mannerisms, is expected out of the context of the social relations of a hospital. Front-stage behaviour relates to the fulfilment of other social roles which are considered informal, in particular, the role of a parent at a children's birthday party. These are people, not roles, who assume a kind and cheerful manner and engage in fun banter and frolic with children. Furthermore, in the context of the social relationship, regarding the activities which occur within the front stage area, performers are said to engage in impression management, controlling how people perceive their social performance. Their presentation is a constructed output within the confines of a self-image or identity they are trying to communicate. Usually, the person closes the area with favourable common social attributes and opens with loose negative values, or the other way around, and is trying to not only persuade but also to help the person see a better reflection of self in the social scape. A balanced self-disclosure is, of course, the best way to go, but many of us, knowing that there is a social contract, assume that people's behaviour is not always the case.

In certain circumstances, people might go backstage, which is an analogy for an area where they can take a break from the demands of being in public. It is a place where they can do, feel, or talk about things that are not considered 'appropriate' for them on the front stage. This difference between the front stage and the backstage is an interrelation of social behaviour that has not been fully understood. Fronts and performances funnel social behaviour as they structure the nature of interactions, the relationships formed, and the realities that are constructed in the social world. Appreciating the concepts outlined in the dramaturgical perspective informs people about the complexity of social life and how they deal with the multiple performances and identities that they assume in the different situations and contexts that they find themselves in.

Management of Roles and Tactics

From this perspective, role management and tactics are equally important parts of social interaction. Goffman's analytical piece delineates sophisticated schemes that people articulate and employ for diverse roles that they have to perform in distinct social situations. Role management is the mental and physical, in some instances, agony that people go through in a bid to assume and fulfil the demands of a particular role as defined by society. Goffman points out that people have many roles, and to cope, they have to manage them effectively, and this often requires shifts to be made between roles.

Still, he emphasises the performative aspect that incorporates his argument that an individual is bound to act out specific behaviours and facial expressions to perform a given role. The ability to take on different roles and manage them is a fascinating contradiction of personal will and socially constructed borders that illustrates the ongoing negotiation of self in a social space. Moreover, role tactics are the mental and behavioural components and strategies that a person uses to manage social situations and control others' thoughts about him or her. The communication of these behaviours and expressions is almost always accompanied and expressed either directly or indirectly, such as through gestures, body disposition, and verbally articulated content. According to Goffman, people use these behavioural frameworks to plausibly defend the balance between the individual masks they assume and the social behaviours expected of them to maintain social order. Goffman argues that people endlessly and intently work on their roles in terms of impression management, which is, in fact, the role they take that the individual acts to design and present constructed images of themselves they deem impressionable. Impression management is a more considered means of communication, and as sometimes outlined, the result of such calculated action is to '...create an impression of themselves in the minds of others which they wish these others to see.' Goffman is the first and probably the only one to stress the role of information, posture, and action people use to arrive at and maintain the impression which they wish other people to have such that they may operate in his or her role effectively. Role tactics and management are more complex than a set of individual actions, as they deeply permeate interpersonal relations and entire systems of organisations.

Group behaviour can involve the performance of roles that require some level of collaboration. It is the cooperative aspect of managing roles in social structures. The same is true for organisations that practice tactical role management to maintain separate organisational identities and cohesive cultures that embody the set values and objectives. The role management and tactics in question offer remarkable knowledge about social life, particularly the tension between the actions of an individual and society. The social life of an individual and the mutual influence between individual actions of every member and society as a whole remain vivid in the work of Goffman, whose Meso theory provides an in-depth understanding of the social structure and social psychology of the individual, which can offer a glimpse into what is yet to be achieved in the field.

Regions, Settings, and Personal Space

To a sociologist, the term 'region' entails more than just a piece of land. Geography is social, and there are social actions that can be performed at certain spaces. The demarcations and use of some personal spaces are very crucial to social exchanges. Goffman's work provides some structure as to how people incorporate some elements of geography in social actions. These include the use of 'front stage' and 'backstage' to elaborate how people control their self-presentation in different areas.

The front stage of a performance has to do with parts that are presented to the public, while the backstage pertains to private individual periods in which a performer can go out of character, unobserved. Also of relevance is the fact that the context of a situation helps determine the nature of social exchange. Different contexts, like a professional workplace, a relaxed restaurant, or a packed underground train carriage, impose their own sociological masks and shapes on how people act and present themselves. These contexts also shape personal space, defined as the zone of space immediately surrounding a person, which was also observed by Goffman as a significant variable in social encounters. Much of the transaction of personal space rests in the distance that people keep from one another as well as factors like orientation and ownership, which are small parts of the larger system that governs everyday social behaviour.

The system of 'civil inattention' also illustrates the extraordinary attention to detail that is characteristically required to manage social encounters in public. Participants in a social setting are tactful while more or less observing the presence of the others and also, most importantly, the privacy that is commonplace in the public. The 'social' in the 'social system' is the pattern of relations and orderly behaviour which concerns a public space, while the 'differentiated' pertains to variety in social space and sociological conditions in which daily life is lived.

A focus on regions and settings as they relate to the human and coupled with an analysis of uneven physical and symbolic spaces helps illustrate the complex ways people negotiate with geographies and create meaning with the surface of the earth and the spaces above.

Impression Management and Facework

The lesson of impression management entails "sponsorship" as described by impression management theorists such as Goffman. These theorists assume from the onset that some behaviours, even subconscious ones, have the purpose of controlling the impressions that people form of them, like exposing the thumbs, and are decided management. It involves the looking-glass self and, to some extent, the social face. Attitudinal behaviours are almost the same as facework closing and facework. Both of them, in large measure, classify the imbalances of social behaviour systems.

In social settings, people try to devise plans and deploy certain behaviours for the sake of impression, which is critical in moulding one's desired self. This could range from how someone dresses, their posture, how they speak, and their overall conduct to their impression. For, in cases when systems are used strategically and controlled to bring about certain outcomes, the system could be the job market, and someone could self-show a controlled system. In the case, in contrast, the demeanour and discourse of self-cautiousness and overwhelming attention to self-control could be self-enactment to the extent of impression formation that in the self is deemed intelligent; the impression or the conduct of exhibiting intelligent behaviour is as a result of self-intentional structures which are much desired to promote that self.

Facework is crucial in the management of self and impression, interpersonal relationships or social control; the control behaviour is aimed at neutralising the intended social impact. It is claimed that such a system is complex because the more orderly the almost tangled social systems are, the more relative the used social structures, self-exposure and self-politeness are, and the smoother the face-saving. When individuals are embarrassed or commit social blunders, they may use humour or self-deprecation to come out of it, demonstrating the touchy nature of facework and social relationship maintenance. The digital age added new dimensions to facework and impression management. Unlike other communications, social media users carefully design their profiles and posts in a bid to create a version of themselves, and in the process, create blurred lines of reality and performance. Also, the problems of facework created by digital communication are a result of the absence of physical communication. This means the user has to be extremely careful and sensitive to the words and accompanying emoticons they use to show they are being sincere and maintaining friendly relations. The concepts of impression management and facework are important for understanding the social interactions and identity construction processes. This understanding sheds light on the complex systems of managing public and private life, and thus, the understanding of human behaviour with its dramatic elements is enriched.

Audience and Interaction

With reference to the dramaturgical perspective, the concept of audience is important for the construction of interaction. It is noted that, in a theatrical show, the audience is important for the shaping of an actor's behaviour and the self-presentation they choose to show. Goffman has made emphasis in this context on the role of the audience.

The dynamics of social interaction evolve fundamentally with the inclusion of an audience whose expectations the individual seeks to satisfy. This illustrates the complexity of social interaction, because the interaction focuses on the audience with the attendant social rules and expectations which must be considered. In addition, the nature and attributes of the audience shape the dynamics of interaction, which makes it necessary for the individual to engage varying tactics in relation to the nature and context of the audience. Even in the most informal occasions, the individual is subject to the self-fulfilling prophecy which dictates the behaviour of performer and audience. From a social behaviour point of view, Goffman comprehensively describes the relationship between performer and audience, elaborating the concepts of performance and audience. Also, even in the ways the audience is perceived, there is an active interaction in which the audience member, in the course of an engagement, relates to the performer. This awareness creates a common social reality through which meaning becomes interactionally derived. Social interaction in the context of the audience is exemplary in describing the fluidity characterising the evolutionary structure of social behaviour.

Therefore, considering the importance of the audience, a theoretical audience would shed light on the social dynamics and construction of social realities, while the audience's impact on the self-presentation of individuals and audience social interaction would outline the analysis of social behaviour and its interaction within a framework of social encounter rather than social behaviour.

Erving Goffman's audience and social interaction Backstage and Confidential Matters

This framework of social interaction under consideration Goffman's analysis allows us to illuminate some aspects of social behaviour in a novel manner. Like in the case of the concept "Backstage and Confidential Matters", people are likely to rationalise the absence of social control as a liberal or "sanitised" form of vertical and oblique supervision. The absence of social supervision is the dial. The naïve representation of the backstage is the area where the individual is perceived as the owner of the self, and the self is as free as a decision as a positive. In the backstage, individuals can shed the skins of their public selves and, in private, do what they would never do in public or what is inconsistent with their social image. This gap is the central theme of this book, which is the shadow created by the audience straining its insurmountable gaze on the individual. Goffman's work reminds us how people in the contemporary world are used to engaging in what is called 'impression management', where people gauge what to share and with whom, or how they share and what information they provide access to.

You do not have permission to access this session, as you have permission to access other settings. There is a place to walk freely, without the restrictions of a social face. Other ethical questions would be what the consequences to social balance would be. Trust, and the possibility of abuse of personal information, is granted. There is this describing the backstage inhibitions of access in all Goffman's works about the impact of the environment and social structure on an individual's attempts to seek authentic relations and assistance. He sheds light on the backstage strands in a social interaction script, which makes it easier to understand the balance of civilised behaviour and the basic drives of individuals concerning the social mask. He offers to look at the framework of social behaviour in new ways. Goffman's theory makes it easier to understand social behaviour and interaction globally. In the next section, other social relations, 'Disruptions and Dramatic Realisation', suggest the breaks in the continuity of flows and the changes in the direction to look at social and individual relations organised in the ribs of the social body.

Disruptions and Dramatic Realisation

In the interaction between people, the disruption functions as the main pivot which enables the accumulation of new social realities and the appreciation of the new order.

These disruptions can take the form of broken front stage behaviours, incompatible conflicts of roles, or unscripted interventions within the boundaries of a particular situation's behavioural contours. In understanding these disruptions, people have to adapt, respond, or realign their behaviours and emotions. This realignment, which behaves like actors attempting to adjust to things going awry on stage, creates excess drama while offering an opportunity for rare glimpses into human behaviour. Disruptions can come from the gaps in a performer's shown self and their disowned, true self, which creates a hurdle to the social validation of their claim. When these discrepancies occur, people face the challenge of coping with the dissonance and deciding which face to wear. This discursive negotiation typically involves tactical manoeuvres that aim to restore balance and equilibrium in the social situation. It also allows for an understanding of the relationship between the performer's private self, the performance they put on in public, and the social order they are trying to maintain. Social order has, more often than not, a commanding structure to it. In many advanced societies, like in the West, this structure demands a loose self that goes on to discredit many aspects of their selves. When a paper is torn, reflexively and immediately, it is divided in two, which we imagine was the intention of the actor performing the behaviour. This analogy applies to why people reflexively attempt to hide the seams of their self. This act is social in nature. It springs from a desire to shield the other from the truth, which is a social mask. And even more, in ruptures, the social self seems to free movements and actions to reveal encumbered and concealed aspects of the social lifeworld.

The illusions of successful presentations contradict the 'front' and 'back' stage distinctions and therefore assist in my understanding of the finer points of impression and self-presentation. The distinctions collapse and illuminate the paradox of the performance within the social structuring of social life. The paradox of social life is resolved by a range of cognitive dissonance and deeply personal systems of social control that manifest as dramatic realisations. During dramatic realisations, there is a cultivated sense of focus and revelation. People start to contemplate their axioms of the social sphere. The analysis, realised as a disruptive social performance, reflexively dissects the social events to the manners in which the 'others' relate, the varied props and contexts in which the self is involved, and the rest of the social scripts. In this context, the analysis of disruptions and dramatic realisations takes centre stage and clarifies a thick description of social life and the social self. The disruptive moments are dramatic and contain lucid details about the paradoxical framework of ordinary existence. Alien to the arbitrary events of life, they can be cut out, as if in a sculptor's block of marble. These moments transform social life.

Concluding Reflections on the Dramaturgical Model

The account of the speaker framework, furthered by Erving Goffman, is rich and deeply insightful in understanding the interrelational aspects of self.

Closing the exploration of the framework, we must also look back on the importance and implications of the dramaturgical perspective. The model explains the manner by which a person shifts and 'performs' in social situations and contexts, as if on a stage. The analogy of actor and stage is revealing, as it centres on social life's fluid and flexible character and gives attention to identity fragmentation and performance dislocation. A notable part of the model is the stress on impression and facework. Through attention to social deference, a person is able to 'relate' his or her self-image to a particular social audience. The imbalance which reflects the identity self-professed as 'personal' is in the same continuum. The work or movement of the person, such as his or her 'theatrical' dressing up and adopting the 'proper' style behaviour, gives enough evidence of perpetual trade and a social rest on these 'different' phases. The concern of the theory is also with regions, or the 'framing' of the space, or the 'setting' and the 'interaction' which reflexively define behaviour in the space.

Realising the broader implications of the perspective, we could also argue that dramaturgical performance is critical to comprehend in practically every profession. In the field of organisational behaviour, leaders could construct their framework for the theory to direct organisational culture and behaviour towards desired and highly productive congruence.

Organisations stand to benefit from a richer understanding of the performative aspects of teamwork that leadership entails, as it broadens their appreciation of the intricacies of interpersonal relations and the accompanying communication methods. In addition, the impression management aspects of performative engagements and their ethically questionable outcomes compel consideration of the power configurations in social situations and the authenticity of manipulation in relation to the exercise of social control over the individual. These questions have significant consequences in the sociological, psychological, anthropological, and communication frameworks and offer new avenues for interdisciplinary scholarship. Today, the interpersonal relations and digital and socially mediated communication framework influence the advancement of the dramaturgical model. Online communication has reshaped self-presentation and audience interaction, creating a new context for the challenges and opportunities of impression management. Appraising the impact of the dramaturgical approach to digital spheres is an invitation to explore the impact of technology on interpersonal relations, communication and the performance of social media identity. In the final parts of the discussion of the dramaturgical model, it is obvious that the essence of the model ranges beyond the initial sociological theories, since it is intertwined with the various ways of interacting with people and the other aspects of life. Goffman's perspective is still an influence on discussions and research by explaining and illuminating the performative dimension of social reality and the artistry of features of social life and impression management. It deepens our comprehension of the complex masks we wear in the performance of daily living.

***

1. **Manning, P. K. (1992).** *Erving Goffman and Modern Sociology.* Stanford University Press.

The book provides a methodical examination of Goffman's dramaturgy, presenting it as a sociological approach rather than a mere metaphor. Manning shows how performance is embedded in institutional routines (e.g., policing, healthcare) and how "fronts" stabilise social expectations.

2. **Fine, G. A. (1993).** *The Sad Demise, Mysterious Disappearance, and Glorious Triumph of Symbolic Interactionism.* Annual Review of Sociology, 19, 61–87. https://doi.org/10.1146/annurev.so.19.080193.000425

Places Goffman's dramaturgy within the broader trajectory of symbolic interactionism. Fine argues that dramaturgy provides a "cultural pragmatics" for understanding how actors negotiate meaning through performance.

3. **Bennett, A. (2018).** *Goffman's Dramaturgy: A Reappraisal.* Symbolic Interaction, 41(1), 105–122. https://doi.org/10.1002/symb.335

A recent critical reassessment that defends Goffman against charges of "theatrical reductionism". Bennett clarifies that dramaturgy is not about deception but about the collaborative, rule-governed nature of social life.

4. **Lemert, C., & Branaman, A. (Eds.). (1997).** *The Goffman*

Reader. Blackwell Publishers.

This essential anthology includes key excerpts from Goffman's works alongside insightful editorial commentary that contextualises dramaturgy within his broader project on the interaction order, stigma, and frame analysis.

5. **Rosenberg, M. (1979).** *Presentation of Self and the Structuring of Social Behaviour*. In M. Rosenberg & R. H. Turner (Eds.), Social Psychology: Sociological Perspectives (pp. 218–243). Basic Books.

Connects Goffman's dramaturgy to identity theory, showing how role performance shapes self-concept and social structure. Emphasises the dialectic between individual agency and social constraint.

6. **Bolton, S. C. (2005).** *Emotion Management in the Workplace: A Dramaturgical Perspective*. In S. Fineman (Ed.), Emotion in Organisations (2nd ed., pp. 122–141). Sage.

Applies Goffman's concepts to organisational settings, especially service work. Shows how employees perform "emotional labour" (à la Hochschild) using dramaturgical techniques to manage customer impressions.

7. **Marwick, A. E., & boyd, d. (2011).** *I Tweet. Honestly, I Tweet Passionately: Twitter Users, Context Collapse, and the Imagined Audience*. New Media & Society, 13(1), 114–133. https://doi.org/10.1177/1461444810365313

Uses Goffman's dramaturgy to analyse social media behaviour. The authors introduce "context collapse"—a digital condition where multiple audiences merge—challenging traditional front/back stage boundaries.

8. **Gregory, D. (1989).** *The Dramaturgical Perspective and the Study of Organisations*. Journal of Management Studies, 26(2), 171–189. https://doi.org/10.1111/j.1467-6486.1989.tb00522.x

Demonstrates how dramaturgy illuminates organisational culture, leadership, and ritual. Shows that "performances" in workplaces are not superficial but constitutive of institutional reality.

9. Burns, T. (1992). *Erving Goffman.* Routledge.

Provides one of the clearest expositions of dramaturgy as a sociological theory (not just a metaphor), linking it to ritual, frame analysis, and the interaction order.

5
Encounters and Rituals
Social Interaction

Beginning Description: Encounters and Rituals

Encounters and rituals are the basis of every social activity and the essence of all social life. This chapter will focus on the primary dimensions of the transactions of social life and the processes of social behaviour controlling the rituals of human behaviour in so-called social life. We are attempting to provide in these pages a deliberated explanation of the specialist dimensions of social life.

The social life of a human being has always been sophisticated and complex, owing to the numerous interdependencies and exchanges of humans. Social sentiments influence these exchanges, imbuing them with meanings. The focus in these pages is on how such encounters and rituals are able to shape the social structure, identity, and control over social conduct.

This is how the subject is approached in this book: using materials from sociology, anthropology, and psychology, an interdisciplinary approach is adopted. Rituals, formal and informal, have existed in all cultures to control social behaviour and even mark a sequence of actions.

Rituals not only connect people together, but also demonstrate the cultural values and belief system of a society through the exchange of salutations and participation in cultural activities. Interactions in social settings have also been studied on a micro level. Everything from social reality to shared meanings includes nuance-filled speech and non-verbal communication. We aim here to untangle the complex system of social interaction through the lens of gestures and movements people use. By emphasising them, we bring to light a new dimension for understanding the multilayered simplicity of day-to-day interactions. This perspective also helps to identify scaffolds from which we can start building pillars of the deep study on how interactions and rituals have profoundly shaped the emergence and integration of social ties and the interplay of personal and social identities.

> Erving Goffman's work on **face-to-face interaction**, **social encounters**, and **interactional rituals** is central to his sociological vision. He viewed everyday social life not as a backdrop to "real" social structures, but as the very site where society is continuously produced, maintained, and negotiated. Key concepts include:
>
> **Encounters**: bounded, co-present interactions governed by tacit rules (e.g., greetings, queueing, eye contact).
>
> **Rituals**: routine, symbolic acts that affirm social bonds and mutual respect (e.g., deference, demeanour, apologies).
>
> **Face-work**: the practices individuals use to maintain their own and others' social "face" (i.e., public self-image).
>
> **The interaction order**: Goffman's term for the autonomous domain of face-to-face conduct, governed by its own norms independent of macro-social structures.
>
> These ideas appear across several of his works, especially:
> - The Presentation of Self in Everyday Life (1959).
>
> - Interaction Ritual: Essays on Face-to-Face Behaviour (1967).

- *Behaviour in Public Places* (1963).

- *Relations in Public* (1971).

The Dynamics of Face-to-Face Interaction

In pondering the activities that civilisation perceives as social, Erving Goffman's theories on face-to-face interaction provide a rich and profound set of intricacies that inform how we conduct ourselves on a daily basis.

   It is through direct social interaction that people active in social life engage in role-taking and impression management while performing acts of social significance. This interaction also includes all the subdivisions of interpersonal communication and , as well, vocal gestures. Goffman attempts to analyse the face-to-face interactions of individuals at a lower level of social contact, aiming to enhance our understanding of the dynamics involved in these micro-level interactions. It is in such interactions that people are engaged in the constant ebb and flow of mutual social positioning. Each interaction serves as a micro setting where individuals can modify, change, and adopt their social identities, allowing for effective self-presentation and adaptation to the social situation. His framework helps us understand the results and outcomes of interactions in which people are engaged in social life and, more specifically, social order when it relies on impression management. In addition, face-to-face interaction is more than just talking to people. It is a more complex system of body movements and gestures, which people may sometimes call body language. Goffman tries to understand how people's movements and the complex of their body parts and their interactions convey to people and social activities, referring to these to their active social functioning. These include socially sensitive and acceptable body movements, ranging from tactful nods of understanding to subtle gestures like suddenly tilting one's head to indicate dominance and control.

Goffman's analysis goes further to focus on the delicate dance of domination and personal space regarding boundaries and face-to-face meetings. The spacing boundaries, whether they are proxemic or putative, overlap as a dance of power and social order. In these activities, people have to centre their attention on the boundaries of their personal space and, further, the rules of their interaction and building relationship modelling to the political social configuration. The addition of the dimension of temporality intrudes complexity on face-to-face meetings. The flow of conversations with their lies in the rhythm and bodily motions, alternating intervals, and overall dance of time (like musical phrases in a sonata) that make the structure and form of meetings. The genius of Goffman easily discerns which action and which by whom, and in what order of syncopation, to outline what they call mutual choreography of meetings, delineating a set of boundaries in relationship coordination and the order of relationship between the participants. Goffman describes voice, touch, and facial expression as additional layers while they space themselves apart or in a conversational rhythm to the classification of them on the shining kaleidoscope of the complex picture of face-to-face interaction. The gist of Goffman's analysis in this context can serve to offer an accessible, yet powerful, way to understand the dynamics of social conduct. His analysis encompasses a wide range of social roles and provides a clear understanding of interaction.

Social norms and structures associated with relationship-building activities

Social structures and norms underpin the focal point of discussion of norms in the contact social context.

The rules and expectations, both explicitly and implicitly, influence behaviour in particular socially defined situations. These rules sustain order and coherence in society by helping set boundaries on social and interpersonal behaviour. In social intercourse, compliance with social norms makes intercourse predictable and fosters understanding of the participants, leading to more effective functioning of social intercourse in a variety of situations. In all situations, social or unsocial, such norms tend to be used to determine acceptable behaviour, to form new relationships, and to exercise social courtesy. In addition, interpersonal social norms are a valuable source of trust and common understanding and of social integration and belongingness in smaller social units. Breaking interpersonal social norms disrupts the harmony of interactions, resulting in social uneasiness, misunderstanding, and the likelihood of a social conflict. Cognisant of such social consequences, people try to employ impression management whereby social behaviour is tailored to the most salient social norms as a means to control given situations. It should be emphasised that social norms and their particular social behaviour prescriptions are not static; they evolve with the culture, the situation, and the context in which social behaviour takes place.

Every person has to adjust to different social environments by modifying their attire, along with their behaviour and speech. Besides, with regard to social norms, their influence does not stop at face-to-face encounters; it extends to other social systems and institutions, colouring wider social systems as well as patterns of collective behaviour. Appreciating the impact of social norms on interpersonal encounters elucidates some aspects of social behaviour and the impact of social cohesion as well as the value of social norms in compliance within engaging and productive social interactions.

Ritualistic behaviours in Everyday Life

The impact of ritualistic behaviours is prominent in shaping our social encounters and experiences. Throughout the day, from the moment we wake up to the time we go to bed, we perform several routine actions that constitute our day. These actions include mundane activities like preparing morning coffee and greetings to coworkers upon arrival at the office, as well as highly formalised practices like family dinners or participation in worship services. When we analyse everyday ritualistic behaviour, the patterns of social behaviour that they exhibit serve different purposes.

They accomplish these goals by establishing boundaries and predictability, allowing people to develop mental maps of their social ecosystems. Additionally, rituals often hold profound meaning, serving as key instruments to emphasise and encapsulate common principles, convictions, and cultural practices. Furthermore, such ritualistic actions assist in the formation and sustenance of relationships. These actions, such as waving at a nearby neighbour, as well as the practices accompanying particular celebrations, strengthen social ties. They enhance continuity and stability in social networks, reinforcing a group's identity and creating social cohesion among the members. Furthermore, the practice of rituals influences the formation of everyday personal and social identities. Individuals actively identify with specific groups, religions, and cultures by engaging in certain behaviours repeatedly. The above rituals strengthen not only individuals' identities, but also the identity of wider social systems by functioning to unify defenders of cultural practices and traditions. Additionally, crossing ritualistic behaviours—in this case, waving to a friend or neighbour and similar customs—highlights an exercise of control and dominance within a social structure.

Ritual phenomena have been shown to reflect existing social power arrangements and institutional behavioural norms, as well as reinforce behavioural norms associated with social power systems. Behaviourists have claimed that the study of daily ritual activities is of paramount significance to understanding the totality of social life and the actions of individuals within it. Studying these rituals teaches us about social and behavioural norms, as well as the behaviour of people in society and the society itself.

Managing social impressions is a phenomenon that is a part of social interactions

Social interactions within society can be defined as part of a complex process taking place within a social setting where 'members' of society are able to associate with each other. Within these processes, individuals can undertake the phenomena that are defined as "managing social impressions and rituals as a part of the social scripts." Individuals undertake both conscious and subconscious efforts to select a relatively favourable social circumstance and present themselves. Goffman postulates that social life revolves around "managing impressions.". His works indicate that people use rituals to create the desired 'impression' of themselves that is advantageous within a 'situation'. Through these works, Goffman demonstrates that an individual has an active role in the impression they create of themselves in their interaction with the surrounding social environment.

Social scripts, or guidance on behaviour expectations in specific contexts, assist these individuals in these endeavours by offering guidelines on appropriate behaviour. Such scripts help determine the norms of behaviour and clarify what actions are expected of a person in a particular situation. Other than self-presentation, impression management also involves understanding other people's behaviours and gestures. Goffman's work sheds light on the subtle patterns in the ways people make sense of other people's actions, often working with tacit agreements over social roles and relationships. The mutualistic impression management in which people actively construct and make sense of each other's presentations illustrates the rather intricate nature of social relations. The management of impressions, self-presentation, and social scripts are, in themselves and in other ways, the product of culture and society. This culture and social structure explains the differences in approaches to impression management and social script behaviour compliance in different cultures and societies. The individual and social context interlink these two factors, warranting a more flexible perspective to understanding them in the context of interpersonal relationships. The social and psychological implications of the outcome of impressions relative to the social structure are complex, particularly self-esteem, social relationships, and mental health.

The ongoing struggle with self-presentation and the need to conform to the expectations of the world brings about stress and anxiety on a personal level. As such, this emphasises the value of this experience in a person's life. In the next part, we will examine the section labelled 'The Importance of Symbolic Acts'. Here, we will discuss the role gesture plays simply to elucidate the parameters of a social situation and to assist in the scaffolding of pre-existing social structures.

The Importance of Symbolic Gesture: Their Use Case in Private Life

A Significance of Symbolic Interactionism describes the essence of meaning behind symbolic interactionism gestures, institutions, and non-verbal communication from face to feet. The concern here is how people communicate emotions, intentions, and attitudes with non-verbal messages. The reception of non-verbal messages and understanding the meaning of these gestures is crucial. To the participant, these actions have some meanings; that is, they are meaningful with regard to culture, society, self, and communication. To appreciate symbolic gestures and actions is to perceive them from their contexts. In social communication, a gentle 'yes', a strong 'yes', a friendly touch, a swift touch, or silence creates and transforms social relationships.

An analysis of culture and communication relating to a culture proves that gestures and their understanding are more than what cultural communication and anthropology describe. It demonstrates boundless social order.

Also, they can use symbolic acts of identity, belonging, and solidarity to tap into social cohesion. They can reinforce common objectives, create social bonds, and indicate inclusion or exclusion of certain members of particular groups. The domain of symbolic acts transcends verbal communication and works as a universal method of communication throughout cultures. However, communication of symbolic acts works for remote activities as well. The complexity is well-articulated with the communication of symbols like emojis, GIFs, and modern-day symbols. All this makes us examine the communication of symbolic acts to understand the identity and social ties they bring forth. Thus, the acts of symbols enable us to understand the relationship between communication and the acts of bonds, mutual understanding, and connection.

Interpersonal Communication and Meaning

Interpersonal communication, as a branch of human communication, is the building block of social ties. The sending and receiving of messages, whether in spoken words or actions, is to send thought and emotion and determine whether an intention is present.

The study of interpersonal communication focuses on the construction, negotiation, and interpretation of meaning in the course of these exchanges to provide the framework of the different facets of human interactions. As a discipline, interpersonal communication is one that is very broad in the different means of its communication. There is the verbal communication that deals with spoken discourse and other linguistic expressions through which a person can think and talk to other people. But the lack of which allows people to interpret the meaning of communication without the need for spoken words to a greater extent because of expressive means of communication like facial expressions and body language. These and other expressive means are considered as signs which are equally as important to understanding communication. It is important to recognise that speech and expression are integral in interpreting interpersonal communication. To say that interpersonal communication is, in its final essence, the communication of meanings does not do justice to its richness. There are many other implicit nuances, layers of meaning, cultural textures, and contextual parameters that are integral in the understanding of interaction. Context, place, and life experiences are some of the many factors that play a major part in the meanings of communication. In addition, the term 'shared meaning' is very important because it helps understand communication and the construction of meaning through negotiation.

Meaning-making in interpersonal communication relates to something much larger in scope, often including aspects of culture that involve power, social identity, and relational positioning in the very act of communication. This in turn underlines the communication difference that exists, explaining how the range of social contexts explains the making and giving of social meaning. This means that the study of interpersonal communication goes beyond the boundaries of individual exchanges to include the contextual geopolitical issues that influence such exchanges. In other words, it is only through the study of interpersonal communication that one is able to disentangle the intricate web of social meaning that is constructed, negotiated, and interpreted within social encounters. It compels us to examine the myriad aspects of social relations, offering a rich understanding of the interconnections that characterise the mundane activities of life while illuminating the intricate interfaces between communication, perception, and social meaning.

Encounters between the individual and society

The encounters between individual actions and the social system are the other key focus of study in sociology. Within the context of encounters and rituals, this focus is particularly important for the understanding of social processes.

An explanation of the interplay phenomena rests on the concept of social agency and the relation of social structure to the relationships, social institutions, and culture influencing a member of a society. For the purposes of this analysis, Goffman provides a starting point on the relation of self and society in face-to-face interaction and in ceremonies. Goffman discusses front-stage and backstage behaviours with the aim of demonstrating how people display indifference to social contexts. This aspect of life interaction highlights the trade-off of self-determination and social rules. Furthermore, in the construction and sustaining of social roles and identities, the individual and society interaction is evident. Encounters entail the formulation and performance of social scripts, and in essence, these social scripts encapsulate the overarching system. These social interactions do not only sustain the prevailing order of society but also possess the capacity to transform it, hence affecting the society as a whole. The society and individual interaction within the society are also illustrated with the construction and sustaining of rituals. Formal or informal rituals are beliefs and values of collectives.

They work to assimilate people into their social circles by cultivating feelings of shared identity and belonging. At the same time, the execution of rituals can also bring to the fore the conflicts between the will of the individual and the will of society, and it can provide perspectives on the relations of dominance and resistance within social formations. The study of the interface between individual and society helps delineate the interplay between micro- and macro-social spheres. It illustrates the delicate balance between individual and social phenomena, the interaction of which is always taken for granted. This framework enhances our comprehension of the interactions of social contexts and individual behaviour, their interpretations, and the enormous complexity of the individual.

Contrasts with Formalised Rituals

In the context of this social canvas, it is important to note the distinction between informal rituals and rituals that have been formalised. While formalised rituals may have particular cultural, religious, or institutional importance, informal rituals can be found woven into the everyday life of human beings. The difference between these two kinds of rituals illustrates to some degree the finer points of social behaviour and the arrangement of society. Formalised rituals generally consist of the doing of particular steps in an order, the use of symbols, and the assumed participation of the group in some form which is a means of expression and reinforcement of cultural traditions.

More informal rituals are characterised by responsive and unplanned actions exhibited in interpersonal contexts that gradually define social bonds and social selves. Whereas formalised rituals are often a set of actions invested with meaning and accompanied by a performative element that is steeped in some traditional structure, informal rituals are much more contextually variable, adaptive, and responsive in form and indicative of daily life. Knowing the characteristics of these two types of rituals is important because they provide clarity to the ways in which social values are reproduced, contested, and transformed. People operate in these two spheres of rituals differently, using structured or formalised rituals for social collective identification and meaning construction, while using informal rituals for social bonding and social role construction. The greater the emphasis on formalised rituals within a social setting, the more complex the social structure seems to be. In a sense, the more informal the rituals are, the more they tend to reflect the underlying social structure, and vice versa. The difference between the two types of rituals offers a more nuanced understanding of the complex interrelations of social life and, in particular, the ways these rituals describe the social structure and, in turn, how these rituals are structured by the social order. The difference and relation these rituals of social life provide highlight the subtle balance between social order and social disorder, no matter the context in which social life is exhibited.

As we explore this, we need to self-reflect as to how the combination of different types of forms of rituals impacts their identity and the people around them.

Conclusion: Social identity impact

Encounters and rituals of different types come as a whole. Understanding social circles from this perspective constructs far richer meanings. In contrast to formal rituals, and the total absence of them, this suggests an elementary level of subtlety and sociality, literally, a drastic impact, through a whole set of invisible yet crucial relations and unsettles, too, collectively. Each person, as we have seen, in every social event, physically attends. Besides having social purposes, every person moves through social expectations, as every normative situation is still part of their social purpose. The very social productivity is edited; hence, the identity periphery is a different construction. A social identity is a composition, so forth and so on, normatively built. A thorough description includes, though does not finish, cultural elements. Societal roles and expectations, social surroundings and setting, and gravity speak to the social order built in the body.

The considerable impact of encounters and rituals is not limited to the social event in question. It ripples through all aspects of life. It is observed that a person collects assumptions, experiences, and feelings of self from all of that, and it is synthesised to the self. The self is not in a self, but all the behavioural, descriptive, and dynamic parts of that. Social identity is how it is perceived. It is, too, a self as feedback and, from the social perspective, is the social identity of the person. Which information does a person have over his or her social identity? Social identity is the answer. It is not socialised by that social identity.

Thus, exchanges and rituals act as fundamental means of negotiation, reinforcement and expression of social identity. The micro- and macro-level implications of these interactions and relationships of influence are considerable. When they are assessed in social identity formation, it is obvious that these processes allow authors of social order and social cohesion to monitor and control it. We also have to keep in mind that social identity dissolution and negotiation in exchanges and rituals may result in discrimination, social identity loss, and unequal social relations. Thus, the need to discuss social identity to understand its impact in broader social contexts becomes the bedrock of the need to understand social division, stereotypes, and discrimination. This also reveals how inclusion might be denied to individuals in a community, and the corresponding denial of dignity and self-esteem is the potential outcome of their involvement in interactions and compliance with rituals. Change, which this understanding permits on the social level, is the advancement of policies that promote interpersonal and structural fairness, equity and social cohesion. Finally, the essence of encounters and rituals focuses on the enduring problem of sociality.

***

1. **Collins, R. (2004).** *Interaction Ritual Chains.* Princeton University Press.

Collins explicitly builds on Goffman (and Durkheim) to develop a systematic theory of how face-to-face rituals generate emotional energy, group solidarity, and social stratification. This is the most influential contemporary extension of Goffman's ritual framework.

2. **Rawls, A. W. (2002).** *Editor's Introduction: Interaction Order and the Problem of Social Order.* In E. Goffman, *The*

Interaction Order: American Sociological Association Presidential Address (pp. 1–30). Reprinted in *Sociological Theory*, 20(3), 269–302.

Rawls, a leading Goffman scholar, contextualises Goffman's concept of the "interaction order" as a foundational but often overlooked alternative to structural-functionalist and rational-choice theories of social order.

3. **Burns, T. (1992).** *Erving Goffman.* Routledge.

Burns provides a thorough intellectual biography, giving significant emphasis to Goffman's examination of encounters and rituals. Burns clarifies how Goffman's micro-sociology challenges macro-theoretical assumptions about agency, structure, and social cohesion.

4. **Manning, P. K. (1992).** *Erving Goffman and Modern Sociology.* Stanford University Press.

The book delves into how Goffman's emphasis on encounters and rituals reorients sociology towards the "micro-architecture" of social life. Manning emphasises the ethical and political dimensions of facial expressions and civility in public spaces.

5. **Goffman, E. (1983).** *The Interaction Order: American Sociological Association Presidential Address. American Sociological Review,* 48(1), 1–17.

Though this is Goffman's own work, it is essential reading and often treated as a standalone theoretical statement. In it, he argues that the interaction order is a distinct domain of social life with its own rules, vulnerabilities, and moral obligations—separate from institutional or societal orders.

6. **Maynard, D. W., & Clayman, S. E. (2010).** *Ethnomethodology and Conversation Analysis.* In G. Ritzer & J. M. Ryan (Eds.), *The Concise Encyclopedia of Sociology* (pp. 211–214). Wiley-Blackwell.

The text demonstrates the influence of Goffman's insights into encounters on the fields of ethnomethodology and conversation analysis (CA). These fields use fine-grained observational methods to study the ritualised structures of talk-in-interaction (e.g., turn-taking, repair, greetings).

7. **Smith, D. E. (1987).** *The Everyday World as Problematic: A Feminist Sociology.* Northeastern University Press.

While critical of Goffman's apparent gender blindness, Smith engages seriously with his encounter framework, arguing that interaction rituals are shaped by power, gender, and institutional hierarchies—thus extending Goffman through a feminist lens.

8. **Tuncay, Z., & Sanders, T. (2022).** *Civil Inattention in the Digital Age: Revisiting Goffman's Interaction Order.* Symbolic Interaction, 45(4), 621–639. https://doi.org/10.1002/symb.628

This is a contemporary empirical study that applies Goffman's concepts, such as civil inattention and ritual avoidance, to urban digital life, demonstrating how smartphones and public space transform traditional encounter norms.

9. **Fine, G. A. (2001).** *Gifted Tongues: High School Debate and Adolescent Culture.* Princeton University Press.

Uses Goffman's ritual and encounter framework to analyse how adolescents perform identity, manage face, and navigate status in competitive speech settings.

6
Stigma and Identity
The "Other" and The "I"

Stigma and Identity

This part summarises the salient aspect and purpose of discussing stigma and identity and prepares for the particulars of such a discussion. When discussing stigma and identity, the analysis goes beyond a simple overview of the interaction, which is quite complex. Stigma significantly influences people's interactions, self-perceptions, and societal perceptions. From a stigma theory perspective, it is important to describe the posited relationships within the macro and micro frameworks of identity. This study attempts to understand the intricacies of identity formation during the socio-psychological process of stigmatisation.

Stigma, in a more sociological context, is the starting point of any analysis of stigma which seeks to understand how particular social divisions are constructed to justify unequal treatment and social subordination. A stigmatisation is the study of social processes which define certain social characteristics as negative and ascribe a social identity (or social identity construction) to those who possess the elements of such social stigmas. Stigma, more than any other phenomenon, reveals the context in which entrenched stigmas and fundamental social principles of a society are obscured, making only the outcomes of stigmatisation by stigmatisers visible. Stigma, in a more sociological context, is the starting point of any analysis of stigma which seeks to understand how particular social divisions are constructed to justify unequal treatment and social subordination. The subject is the study of social processes, which define certain social characteristics as negative and ascribe a social identity (or social identity construction) to those who possess the elements of such social stigmas.

People inch through harsh terrains moulded by social biases and stigmatisers, biases which result in a gradual but dangerous loss of identity. A crucial element in untangling the plight of the stigmatised is in the psychological and social dynamics of the stigma. There is a need to ponder the frameworks and strategies individuals employ when coping with stigma because they shed light on resilience and self-determination. It involves the imprisonment of collective actions dictated by stigma in the realms of self-advocacy and self-determination, reconstructing the stigma socialised by the dominating society. Stigmatisation is more intense at the intersection of various marginalised identities, which broadens the need to focus on the incorporation of different social stratification systems. It is called intersectionality. The focus of this work is on the case studies describing the experiences of people who suffer from stigma. The aim is to arouse sympathy, understanding, and biases and correct the false beliefs around stigma. This work concludes with a reflection on its overall themes and prepares the reader for new parallel discussions about institutions and totality. The point is to understand the totality of the work in respect to stigma and self-identity.

The Conceptual Framework of Stigma

Stigma is based on the concepts of "othering" and dangerousness, which are part of the "dis" category. Stigma, therefore, involves the "othering" of an individual and a distorted understanding of that individual, portraying them in discrediting and dangerous terms. Being dangerous to others is a complex, and therefore, multi-determined phenomenon. It has, in fact, many layers of meaning.

Stigma consists of broad and interlinked elements on the social, psychological, and cultural levels. Stigma is the associational labelling and discriminatory stereotyping of people or social formations on the basis of differences from social norms. A large part of the understanding of stigma as a complicated social phenomenon is attributed to the works of Erving Goffman. Goffman describes how stigmatised people literally shrink from society as they struggle with their most mundane day-to-day interactions and self-identification. In Goffman's case, the internal struggle with a 'spoilt' or 'stigmatised' identity becomes the most difficult challenge. A person with these spoilt identities' undergoes a tremendous amount of discrediting and devaluation. To be devalued is not the opposite of being valued but rather being spoilt valued or being filed under a social category, losing the vantage point of having unique social traits. Goffman's work examines how social institutions and powers stigmatise individuals and use these stigmas to perpetuate social stigma. Social phenomena related to stigma shape each individual's reality. Individuals and small groups do not construct stigma solely based on their experiences. These are deeply rooted social notions that are associated with hierarchy, institutional control, and social limitations in the practice of those norms.

Analysing macro-level factors such as systemic discrimination and culture in micro-level processes as they pertain to the realities of the lives of valued but stigmatised persons is crucial. Seeing stigma in a socially and culturally stigmatised context points out the need to understand various manifestations and consequences of stigma.

Furthermore, Goffman's social framework highlights the active, "...performative..." aspects of stigma, which reveal the impression management and self-presentation tactics employed by persons with stigma in the management of their stigmatised identities. The performative aspect of stigma underlines the broader context, indicating that stigmatised individuals must navigate and attempt to conform to the numerous expectations and prejudices of an unaccepting society. Goffman's focus on the '...slipperiness and variability of the processes of stigmatization....the myriad stigmatisation...' is an invitation for description which notes the social and structural constraints on self-defined, '...stigmatised peoples...'stigmatisation...' active ... active and resilient responses.

Goffman's conceptualisation of stigma, which posits stigma as a multi-layered continuum, enhances his view that the individual is at the centre of a web of social relations, a concept that cultural representation partially describes. Such a view, which states that '...the individual is a centre of a web of social relations', emphasises the importance of understanding the social layers that influence an individual's relationships, stigma, and identity. It focuses on them. It emphasises the stigma that is socially and culturally charged against individuals. stigmatised identity and geopolitics of identity stigmatised identity, such as in the multi-border, socio-culturally fractured context of diaspora. Goffmanian interpretations of stigma serve as foundational texts for subsequent works that address the severe consequences of social closure, identity, and stigma on both individual and collective human health.

Historical Perspectives on Stigma

Stigma is associated with a long and complex history of societal, cultural, and institutional beliefs, attitudes, and practices.

The history of stigma dates back to ancient cultures where people suffering from some form of physical deformity or illness were often shunned by societies. During ancient Greece, people exhibiting visible disabilities were considered an inferior subgroup of society and, as such, were often socially isolated. This stigma enabled people to maintain visible difference discrimination throughout history. During the Middle Ages, stigma became intimately connected to acts of religious moral condemnation. Non-conforming individuals were often labelled as heretics, witches, or, at best, sinful, and as such, were socially isolated and treated brutally by societies. Stigma became part of social control as part of early modern medicine, where many illnesses and conditions were simply thought to represent moral decay or divine retribution. This cruel mix of religious zeal, superstition, and medical ignorance led to the suffering of many innocents. With the onset of the Industrial Revolution, new forms of stigma as a social control became apparent. Socioeconomic inequalities, large-scale illness, urbanisation, and the rapid growth of some cities enabled the classification of an entire group as morally degenerate or socially obnoxious. Even today, society continues to practise and perpetuate these deep-rooted stigmas.

To appreciate the social impact of stigma, one must first

analyse how the stigma of a phenomenon has evolved and how it continues to change, adapting to the specificities of one's contemporary society.

Structural Sources of Stigmatisation

Stigmatisation encompasses legal, political, and cultural aspects, which are reflected in the remnants of society's cultural fabric, economy, and contemporary politics. Speaking of politics, policies, and laws, they form and structure the political remnants of the past that serve to discriminate against people. With regard to the economy, it is essential to note that negative social biases, which often accompany submerged multi-faceted stigmas of social injury, are most integrated at lower sets of the socio-economic folkloristic echelon. A society where the economy is stratified, stigmatising stereotypes, and the wealth is stigmatising stereotypes is often termed a 'Piscean society', where the stigmatising zenith is the apparition of overshadowing 'tailless stones' within the civilisation lost in the chasm of the ocean, with a multi-faceted society luxuriating above.

Moreover, a society that is infatuated with the chasm of the ocean is termed a cultured society, whereas a civilisation that luxuriates above is termed an industrial society. As civilisation reaches its peak, it is essential to reduce the separated strata through interdisciplinary approaches.

'Otherness' and stereotypical thinking can be fostered by differential presentation and representation. Furthermore, by endorsing and passing on biased beliefs and values, religious, educational, and family systems can act as vehicles for stigmatisation. Additionally, the design of social institutions like healthcare, criminal justice, and education may include biassed and stigmatising practices that create unequal opportunities for individuals who experience stigma. These structural sources of stigmatisation need to be identified and explored to mitigate the omnipresent impacts of stigma on individuals and communities. By clarifying the matrix of sociopolitical structures that sustain stigma, we can advocate for social reconstruction and transform stigmatising social arrangements.

Identity Formation under Stigma

Identity formation is complex and involves numerous processes, and stigma can be a determining factor in this development. Stigmatisation alters the way individuals think and formulate their identity in their social world. Stigma gives rise to self-images that are negative and overly self-sensitive, in which case positive, integrated identities become very difficult to construct.

In this section, we dive more depth into the relationship between stigma and identity and the issues pertaining to an individual's identity, particularly covering the issues related to stigma.

The identity formation process consists of the integration or synthesis of self-lived experiences and interactions within life's circumstances and the cultural expectations of the community to which he or she belongs. However, the introduction of stigma to this process creates a mental block or a stampede. Stereotyping and discrimination resulting in stigma create an intricate situation where the individual feels devalued either socially, politically, or economically, or even, for some people, in all these aspects. Feeling ashamed or disappointed in oneself, resulting from this, leads the empath to try to understand how alien he or she feels towards the surrounding society.

The self-stigma, or the internally applied stigma, permeates the process of identity formation in a unique way that Goffman describes in the concept of 'spoilt identities'. The individual defines themselves in relation to their differences or flaws, and in this process, they are identified by stigma. A spoilt identity results from the inability or failure to achieve a cohesive and supportive environment, exposing the individual to relentless negative feedback.

The interplay of stigma and identity and their intersection considers and involves other aspects of diversity: race, gender, sexual identity, and even disability. Other established identities lead to both the formation of stigma and the development of further stigmatisation, along with enhanced complexity that causes distress.

Take, for example, individuals living with multiple, overlapping stigmas. Their efforts, however, are compounded by the additional burden of having to negotiate stigma, which adds another dimension of complexity to an already intricate process of identity formation. This complexity further highlights the difficulty of dealing with stigma, the multiplicity of its constituent elements, and how identity intertwines with stigma.

A profound understanding of stigma and its formation, especially as a complex phenomenon with social and psychological dimensions, can greatly aid in identifying potential coping strategies for the resultant stigma, particularly its internalised and self-imposed forms like resilient identity. These coping and resilience strategies, such as stigma self-management, serve to ease and soften the control that stigma exerts on the individual. Social support and affirmative networks can, more importantly, assist in the positive construction of identity under stigma.

These are the strategies we encounter that help us understand stigmas and their effects on identity while dealing with social stigma. The purpose of these strategies is to help understand and demonstrate how stigma and social identification can significantly impact, or even completely control, an individual.

Identity construction, especially under the weight of stigma, anchors the identity of social interaction and the socially narrated life of the individual, as this section on stigma and identity formation seeks to clarify. It is a complex phenomenon and one that we have not documented very well. There is a fear that identities are too readily and easily fixed in a simplistic and emotional manner. Understanding how identity is constructed on such an aggressive, even malevolent, and angelic face of stigma illuminates profound depths that not many individuals have the effort to comprehend.

The self-driven tenacity alongside the stigma attached to the identity formation that surrounds them shines through in the case study.

The psychological and social impacts of stigmatisation

The effects of stigmatisation on the psyche and society as

a whole are deep-rooted and multi-faceted, and they profoundly impact people and populations on a micro and macro level. Psychologically, the burden of stigma inflicts feelings of shame, guilt, and a decline in self-worth. Stigma, the negative perception society forms and acts upon, leads to self-imposed feelings of inadequacy, self-doubt, and a myriad of possible mental health issues as a result. In addition to mental health issues, stigma breeds a sense of loneliness and isolation through the decimation of social connectedness. Psychologically, the stagnant sense of internal imbalance has a debilitating impact on the general functioning of the entire system. Socially, the impact of stigmatisation results in the continuation of discrimination and social disparity, as the stigmatised are subjected to a myriad of obstacles in obtaining education, employment, health care, and other services. These barriers not only serve to limit the economic and social growth of the individual in question but also vastly serve to widen the gaps of bias and discrimination in society. In addition to separating the stigmatised from the rest of society, the consequences of stigma, and its extension, are not isolated to the individual. It has deep-rooted consequences on the family, social life, and community. Stigmatisation results in the erosion of social capital, social cohesion, and trust in the community; it distances people and fractures families. It can even escalate the fear of stigma, trigger self-censorship in certain aspects, and hinder authentic and valuable communication and social interactions.

Stigmatisation stunts social progress and unity, thereby weakening and dividing the social fabric. The psychological and social repercussions of stigma require a broad-based response anchored on education, social activism, reformist and aligned policies, and stigma-focused social support. Cultivating a climate of stigma-free understanding, support, inclusiveness, and empowerment is the best way to address the negative impacts of stigma and stigma-reduction regions where the individual's dignity is fully respected and appreciated. Stigma thrives out of the discriminatory practices, set empathy, and, more generally, negative attitudes that society holds. Systematic efforts to address these attitudes would advance society to a more just and humane place where the negative impacts of stigma do not hinder the growth of human potential.

Managing Stigma: Strategies and Adaptations

Due to the impact of stigmatisation on individuals and communities, there is a need to develop efficient strategies to cope with and manage the challenges that come with stigma. We have analysed a range of strategies and adaptations that individuals and society develop to address the challenges of living with stigma.

These strategies cover a broad range, from personal psychological coping to organised community efforts that combat stigmatisation to assist the community. Stigma, and the stigma attributed to a person from a socially defined group, is not only a social phenomenon but also an individual phenomenon. Stigma coping strategies also depend on the subjective social status and the hierarchy of the stigmatised group among different agents in society. Stigma, and more specifically the social, the more social, the more stigma, arises out of the social processes of its generation as the cultivation of social sympathy.

People undergoing stigmatisation usually use communicative reframing and positive dissociation identity techniques, accompanied by stigma transcendence. Moreover, the creation of social and safe space support networks can be critical for individuals to tell their stories and strategise collaboration to combat stigma. On the social level, different kinds of advocacy and educational campaigns are important ways to counter stigma and achieve social change.

These programmes help to raise the profile of stigmatised individuals and provide the community with the opportunity to develop a deeper sense of empathy and understanding. Additionally, and perhaps most importantly, legal and policy reforms help to eliminate the systemic sources of stigma by providing all members of society with equal access and opportunities. Adaptations to stigma may also take the form of countercultural stories with the intention of celebrating and legitimising deeply marginalised identities.

From art and literature to community-based activism, these cultural forms are ways of exercising agency and honouring the stigma-bearing experiences. By seeking to transform the hegemonic narratives, these forms of creation challenge stigma and, simultaneously, open the gates for more complex and varied understandings of many identities. Finally, the complexity of stigmatised identities requires specific and multilayered approaches that take the web of subjugation into account.

Developing effective strategies to combat stigma requires an understanding of how its different forms converge and accumulate. The dense reality at the intersection of multiple marginalised identities motivates stigma-critical work, and an analysis of the differing tactics and strategies of stigma management reveals much about the strength and self-determination of individuals and communities. The artistry of personal strategies and group efforts, activism, and the culture of stigmatised people reflect the hope for dignity and self-determination, which is the essence of the struggle against stigma.

Case Studies in Stigmatised Identities

We will focus on specific case studies which highlight the dilemmas and complexities that come with stigmatised identities. These case studies will demonstrate how stigma operates in different social situations and how it interacts with different aspects of identity. With these examples, we hope to illustrate the reality of stigma and the consequences that come with it to expand our understanding of the complexity of stigma.

Case Study 1: The Transgender Experience Deepening our knowledge of the transgender experience will highlight the challenges and achievements of people with untold gender identities in an environment characterised by bias and bigotry.

Focusing on the multiple stigmas associated with the transgender population, we can evaluate the social paradoxes and structures regarding the adversities encountered and the range of resilience and agency exerted to secure acceptance and affirmation.

Case Study 2: Mental Health and Stigma In the more nuanced analysis of the stigma attached to mental health, we will examine the tremendous toll mental illness stigma takes on people's self-concept, their resources, and their general wellness. In telling the stories of people with mental health issues, we want to change the dominant narrative and stigmas, and we want to fight for the stigmatised to have more moral support when it comes to mental health issues.

Case Study 3: Racial Identity and Stigmatisation In this particular case, we will focus on the realities of the people subjected to racial stigmatisation and the consequences of enormous structural discrimination. By examining the phenomena of racial stigmatisation, we hope to bring to the surface the historical and current inequities of the geography along with the dominant discourses on racial identity and attempt to provide the people who suffer from racial stigmatisation agency to speak for themselves, while analysing the societal structures that allow such discrimination to continue.

Case Study 4: Disability and Social Stigma

Studying the stigmatisation of disability opens up the external barriers faced by persons with disabilities, such as societal attitudes, structural barriers, and discrimination. Through understanding the disability and stigma nexus, we wish to foster understanding of the rich tapestry of individual narratives and experiences of persons with disabilities to promote advocacy and inclusive action to combat discrimination.

These case studies will help illustrate the rich and complex nature of stigmatised identities and deepen understanding of the lived realities of persons with disabilities stigmatised on more than one level, thus revealing the need for action in society.

Intersectionality and Compound Stigmas

An example of intersectionality can be found in the systems of disadvantage and discrimination in social categorisations such as race, gender, class, or sexual orientation. Social categorisations are a defined and constituent part of discrimination systems. Stigmatised identities, such as the intersectionality felt in this case, speak to how a person suffers from several forms of stigma at the same time.

Legal scholar Kimberlé Crenshaw first defined the concept of intersectionality in relation to the unique position of Black women. In her work on Black feminism, Crenshaw observed that women faced patriarchal oppression, and women of colour experienced both patriarchal and racial oppression. Feminism and anti-racism in her time did not consider her situation, what Crenshaw calls intersectional oppression.

Since then, the concept of identity and social positioning has expanded to include a number of other dimensions. People with intersecting marginalised identities experience unique and compounded forms of stigma and discrimination that cannot be understood by analysing individual facets of identity in isolation. A person of colour who identifies as a part of the LGBTQ+ community, for instance, faces a different set of challenges than one who identifies as a person of colour or as a part of the LGBTQ+ community. When different stigmatised identities are combined, they produce a set of specific vulnerabilities and barriers that inhibit full participation in society, also known as social inclusion. To address and lessen systemic inequities, understanding compound stigmas is essential.

Recently, scholars and activists have called attention to the need to understand and address compound stigmas in the healthcare system, criminal justice, employment, education, and other fields. Focusing on the experiences of people with multiple marginalised identities allows for the proliferation of targeted strategies, which are more likely to be effective because of the complexities involved in the realities of people's lives. This intersecting form of discrimination, or stigma, has been described as intersectionality. It is a reminder that identity and existence can be more complicated than they may appear. Furthermore, it is apparent that the experience of stigma is non-monotonous and, in fact, varied and complex, especially in relation to the interplay of social identities.

To aid in the understanding of the implications of the concepts in total institutions, it is important to add an intersectional approach to the understanding of the dynamics of stigmatisation and identity within an institution.

Conclusion and Transition to Total Institutions

Intersectionality and compound stigmas explain the complexities of interlocking forms of stigma and how they interact with someone's identity. We now must conclude the discussion on stigma and identity and turn to total institutions. Total institutions offer a different perspective on how the stigma and identity dynamics can be explored. These institutions hold a captive clientele in a controlled environment with total regulatory control over all aspects of their existence. This view offers an alternative perspective on the dynamics of stigmatisation and how personal identity is shaped. Total institutions and the interlocking compound stigmas offer a unique understanding of the dynamics of social oppression and the resilience and vulnerabilities of individuals. As uncovered in previous chapters, total institutions allow us a unique way to examine the bonded stigma and identity interactions in those settings. This is where I feel the framework of total institutions is most useful. We can examine how total institutions further stigmatise individuals and the resultant shaping of their identity.

Further, studying the coping strategies utilised by people in total institutions shows how such institutions can pay attention to the pervasive forms of stigmatisation. Learning the plight of people with multi-layered stigmas placed upon them in total institutions adds to the understanding of the nuanced relationships between stigma and identity and how such knowledge can be used to create a more empathetic and inclusive society. An integrated assessment of these issues enhances our understanding of the complex ways stigma is woven into identity construction and serves to strengthen the case for advocacy on behalf of the people who are most vulnerable. In the next chapters, we will step into the world of total institutions and examine the stigma and identity construction process in these closed social systems.

***

Link, B. G., & Phelan, J. C. (2001). *Conceptualising Stigma.* Annual Review of Sociology, 27, 363–385. https://doi.org/1

0.1146/annurev.soc.27.1.363

This foundational article expands Goffman's ideas into a modern sociological framework, emphasising power, labelling, and social context.

Pescosolido, B. A., Martin, J. K., Lang, A., & Tuch, S. (2008). *Rethinking the Stigma Construct: Integrating a Modified Goffman Framework with the Stress Process Model.* In T. P. Thornberry (Ed.), *Advances in Criminological Theory: Taking Stock: The Status of Criminological Theory* (Vol. 15, pp. 273–302). Transaction Publishers.

Integrates Goffman's insights with psychological stress models to examine how stigma affects mental health.

Crocker, J., Major, B., & Steele, C. (1998). *Social Stigma.* In D. T. Gilbert, S. T. Fiske, & G. Lindzey (Eds.), *The Handbook of Social Psychology* (4th ed., Vol. 2, pp. 504–553). McGraw-Hill.

This comprehensive review contextualises Goffman within social psychological theories of identity and prejudice.

Stafford, M. C., & Scott, R. R. (1986). *Stigma, Deviance, and Social Control: Some Conceptual Issues.* In S. C. Ainlay, G. Becker, & L. M. Coleman (Eds.), *The Dilemma of Difference: A Multidisciplinary View of Stigma* (pp. 77–91). Plenum Press.

This work critically examines Goffman's conceptualisation of stigma in relation to deviance and social control.

Parker, R., & Aggleton, P. (2003). *HIV and AIDS-related Stigma and Discrimination: A Conceptual Framework and Implications for Action.* Social Science & Medicine, 57(1), 13–24. https://doi.org/10.1016/S0277-9536(02)00304-0

Applies and extends Goffman's framework to public health, especially in the context of HIV/AIDS.

Deacon, H. (2006). *Towards a Sustainable Theory of Health-Related Stigma: Lessons from the HIV/AIDS Literature.* Journal of Community & Applied Social Psychology, 16(6),

418–425. https://doi.org/10.1002/casp.900

The article discusses the limitations and utility of Goffman's model in contemporary health stigma research.

Tyler, I. (2020). *Stigma: The Machinery of Inequality.* Zed Books.

The book offers a critical sociological re-reading of Goffman, situating stigma within the context of neoliberal governance and structural inequality.

Scambler, G. (2009). *Health-related Stigma.* Sociology of Health & Illness, 31(3), 441–455. https://doi.org/10.1111/j.1467-9566.2009.01162.x

The article builds on Goffman's work by proposing a "stigma-alliance" model, which emphasises the role of power and social structure.

7
Total Institutions
Prisons, Mental Asylums, Barracks, Monasteries, etc.

What is meant by Total Institutions?

Confined structures, societal frameworks, and human behaviours are better understood within the 'Total Institutions' boundaries defined by Erving Goffman and explained through his 'Asylums' work. It includes features and environments where people work and live under one authority and undergo drastic changes to their routines. He defined boundaries comprising prisons and mental asylums, barracks, and even monasteries as total institutions. He also described regimentation, surveillance, personal will loss, and autonomy loss as key components.

Such types of institutions are described as total institutions and elicit an emphasis on the control an institution exercises on an individual's life, dominating their activities and even basic necessities. Such forms of complete dependence on the institution demonstrate control dominance as exemplary. Goffman delves into power configurations intertwined with processes of socialising and personal self-systems fossilised within closed borders. It is necessary to highlight the change components that total institutions illustrate, particularly the changes within the entities confined to these institutions and the systems that enabled total institutions to come into existence.

This chapter will explore and analyse the defining principles of total institutions and how they define and impact human life and interactions.

Defining Features of Total Institutions

Total institutions encompass a unique form of social structures that profoundly affect the lives of people within them. The unique features of total institutions are unlike any other form of institution, and appreciating these features is crucial in understanding the magnitude of their impact on human experience. Within the jurisdiction of a total institution, an individual encounters an overwhelming claim of dominion and jurisdiction. Every single day and in every undertaking, one is governed in matters of the allocation of time and space, the conduct of permissible actions, the sensing of communication, and the behaviour that they are allowed to manifest. This control is not solely restricted to the conventional levels of governance and administration; it extends to virtually every aspect of private life and individual social mechanics. It is this domineering control that functions to construct and sculpt the personalities of people imprisoned within these institutions. Additionally, the geographical boundaries of total institutions serve to hold the bodies of their occupants and limit them.

The elimination of space and distance from the larger community facilitates an inward-focused environment that cultivates its own ideologies, practices, and systems. Moreover, the physical setting encourages extreme physical and social withdrawal and the development of an independent social system and culture that is often in stark contrast to the surrounding society. In total institutions, individuals surrender an enormous amount of personal freedom, domain, and choice, and instead, submit to rule, self-discipline, and the autonomous systems of an institution that govern myriad aspects of their existence. The rationale being that their existence is suspended in an institution, triggering an inner self-questioning and an inability to withstand the external elements that, in other conditions, is termed a loss of control and instead is cultivated, in this case, as dependency. These attributes enable a total institution to deeply influence the conduct, behaviour, and attitude of individuals in their possession, making total institutions some of the most powerful entities in the world.

The Role of Power and Dominance

Within total institutions, individuals' daily lives and the relationships they can form are greatly circumscribed. Power and dominance are factors of total control, that is, control that is absolute. Power is afforded to the personnel of the institution who are in charge and whose function is to execute the control of the order, to rule behaviour, and to hand down punishment. The rule and the behaviour that is to be controlled encompass anything and everything that relates to the lifetime of an inmate, from everyday practices to the routines that are part of the structural framework of that society, how an inmate ought to be functioning in that setup and the order, as well as the systems that govern the society which offer some form of social control.

The total institution commands dominion and warps and serves no less than a dozen functions. It forms a line of systems which several aspects of the core functions of the institution reward and punishment systems, order and discipline. It also reinforces the broader social order. In addition, the constancy of dominion and total control fosters environments in which personal liberty is severely restricted and absolute obedience to the total institution's rules and regulations rather becomes the law of the land. In the context of total systems, dominion also alters the workings of the interpersonal relations between officers and inmates. It modifies the workings of the institutional order and the system of governance. The use of dominion serves to rationalise and control social and structural order, resulting in social relations which derive dominion. The strength dominion serves, with total control, is ever present in the institution's order system of social relations. dominion and their impacts A dominion institution cannot equally be a social climate order. The construction of social order dominion is altered to be understated. The control is pervasive and total. It leads to the inmates losing their sense of disenfranchised subjective feeling to dominion inner control of personal agency. It is also accompanied by more severe mental dominion of inmates' control and dominion of the officers' inner relations between the dominion of social power of the institution.

Grasping the fine points of authority and control within total institutions borders on critical to understanding the impact of incarceration on the wellness of the individual, as well as the implications for society as a whole. It raises fundamental issues concerning the ethics of social relations and the obligations for reforming institutions. Therefore, a fundamental understanding of the authority and control a system can yield serves as a prism through which to discern the complexities of total institutions and the near unfathomable implications on the human condition.

The Social Structure and Dynamics of Inmates

Within total institutions, the social structure of inmates is intricate as well as interwoven with relationships, power, and social orders that define the behaviour and experience of confined individuals. We seek to clarify the social structure and dynamics within total institutions to catch the norms, roles, and behaviours. At the most basic level of inmate social structure is the construction of cliques, which provides a feeling of safety, support, and belonging within a controlled environment. Social bonds, within total institutions, are coping mechanisms that help ease the control, uncertainty, and surveillance. Additionally, the very nature of the control and dominion residing in the power relations of these social systems ends up determining the extent of privileges, resource accessibility, and the decision-making roles of the inmates. The social order is at least in part defined by the hierarchies which derive from longevity and social status, and is further shaped by social relationships so as to then define the behaviour and interaction of persons in the confined setting.

On the other hand, the social structure of inmates and the consequences of institutionalisation on the individual self and self-concept are interdependent. Individuals within the total institution social structure assume a variety of roles, engage in a range of actions, and follow the unspoken normative behavioural standards of the inmate society. The construction of identity in these circumstances is primarily in terms of the desire to be part of a group, to be safe, and to freely exercise a portion of the control and order over the entire structure.

Crucial to the construction of the social structure of inmates segregated into the various categories is the study of the social structure of an inmate in total institutions, which is more so an informal economy. The social system within the total institution is characterised by various self-contained barter exchange systems, informal trade networks, and even a complete underground economy which controls trade in the goods, services, and even money independent of the total institution.

This section will focus on the social conflicts, alliances, and the overall infrastructure of relationships of inmates, which, while analogous to societal relationships in many aspects, would contain entirely different nuances due to the nature of total institutions. It is only through gaining an understanding of the social structures within total institutions that one can appreciate the breadth of the realities of life within them.

Behaviours that are both adaptive and maladaptive

Within the framework of total institutions, an individual is likely to display both adaptive and maladaptive behaviours as an outcome of the particular behaviours that the system, and the system-controlled environment, permit. Adaptive behaviours, otherwise known as strategies of coping, are all the techniques that an individual employs in order to 'live' within an institution. It can be the compliance with institutionally imposed regulations, cooperation for the purpose of alliance in social relationships with other inmates, and other attempts to produce an environment that would be predictable in both its nature and arrangement. In contrast, maladaptive behaviours are all reactions that are either self-defeating in nature or such that they hinder the proper functioning of a system. These self-defeating strategies can include, but are not limited to, depression, anxiety, resistance to social communication and relationships, self-infliction of injuries, or resistance to the social system and its structures as a whole.

Reconciling adaptive and maladaptive behaviours and their implications on total institutions is important and tells us how these behaviours serve to uphold or disrupt order. There is literature, including field research, attesting to the collection of adaptive and maladaptive behaviours in total institutions. Some individuals display extreme resilience and adaptability, bordering on creative problem-solving. They might form peer support networks, participate in constructive activities, and find ways to exercise agency despite the institution's restrictions. Others, however, express maladaptive behaviours due to their struggles with losing autonomy and their identity. They might become rebellious, lose their personal and social identity, or become emotionally and psychologically troubled and develop resistance and oppression. The adaptive and maladaptive behaviour phenomenon in total institutions speaks to the configurations of personal agency and institutional counter-agency. In addition, it tells us important, more general rationales on how individuals in total institutions work out their situations.

Examining factors such as shifting gender roles, ageing, subculture, and social class assists the entire research scholars to appreciate the nuances of the total institution phenomenon.

Processes of Institutionalisation

The process of institutionalisation fundamentally alters the experience of those crammed into total institutions. It refers to the forced integration of people into an institution's culture, daily activities, and standard expectations. It can alter the thinking, feelings, and actions of a person in a profound manner. One of the features of institutionalisation is its ordered setting. It controls every minutia of a person's life, such as waking hours, leisure, and social interactions. This can cause a decline of free will and personal choice, as that person will become reliant on the institution for fundamental items as well as self-affirmation. Additionally, absolution amnesia occurs when a person leaves the institution due to their internalisation of the rules and practices deemed acceptable there. Moreover, the dominating features of total institutions suppress the freedom of self-governance. The person tends to have a submissive disposition and becomes apathetic towards self-governance.

Such actions can encourage a cycle of increasing centrality that reinforces the institution's values. Total institutions can also perform processes of socialisation that integrate the newcomer into the problematic constellation of behaviour and belief patterns in the institution through both direct and indirect mechanisms. Furthermore, the relations of social definition and social treatment of people in the institution can further their institutionalisation, as they are largely characterised and responded to regarding their roles in the institution and not in the light of their personal attributes. There are immediate and remote effects of institutionalisation on the individual, particularly on their self-image, self-control, and functioning when released from the institution. Comprehending the varied and complex processes of institutionalisation can assist in formulating strategies to address the concerns of people living in total institutions as well as construct mechanisms that facilitate their primary reintegration into the social fabric.

The Effects of Institutionalisation on One's Identity and Self-Perception

In the case of total institutions, the effects on one's identity and self-perception are greatly impacted; a well-known example lies in the work of Erving Goffman. His work discusses how people are more susceptible to these processes and are exposed to institutionalisation in a way that change is permanent.

The separated nature of these institutions involves procedures that enable institutions to yank away the roles and social identities of individuals and brand them with the tags of prisoners and the institutionalised. The absence of the external indicators of identity can go on to create a primal feeling of dislocation and confusion as the individuals struggle with the collapse of self-concept and relinquished social roles. Moreover, total institutions that focus on constant surveillance and scrutiny of inmates tend to expand the scope of the dehumanisation process, compelling individuals to perceive and understand themselves as inmates within the system. This depth of imbalance of power renders a portion of self a mark of captivity and a passive constituent of the system, reinforcing the circle of self vis-à-vis the institution. This circumscribed freedom, coupled with the intermingling undercurrents of the institutional routine, alters one's self-perception as the demands of the institution take precedence. Beyond the period of institutionalisation, the effects of total institutions on identity and self-perception significantly impact the psychological and emotional state of the individual.

Inmates transitioning back into society have to face a lot of challenges, like feelings of isolation, stigma, and losing their self-identity. Inmates carry a lot of self-blame that makes them have a tough time trying to reconcile their identities and the stigmatising things that are attached to their past. Furthermore, the impact of the time spent in the institution continues to affect their entire post-incarceration life. Those individuals constantly have to face issues with their sense of agency, trust, and authority. This phenomenon is due to the blurred feeling of control that results from being in such institutions. The focus of this analysis is to uncover the various concepts of identity and self within deeply bounded structures. This study is framed around the idea of the impact of institutionalisation on identity. The results of such confinement and regulation showcase the primal understanding that is needed to appreciate the implications of such institutions and their impacts on people at a profound psychological level.

Comparative Analysis with Other Institutions

When working on the concepts of total institutions, it is

crucial to carry out a comparative analysis with other types of institutions to assess and clarify their unique features and operating systems.

The distinctions between correctional facilities, military barracks, and educational boarding schools readily reveal the differing power relations, social orders, and levels of freedom afforded these various contexts as compared to total institutions. Such institutions, as we shall see, assert control of an unparalleled kind over the myriad aspects of an individual's life and render him or her, in a profound sense, utterly dependent on the institution for the entirety of existence, as well as for the routines of sustenance, activity, social contact, and interaction. Such institutions serve, in a way, to furnish an example of the utter control and the monotonous routines which, for as yet unknown reasons, seem to be missing from the other forms of institutions. Furthermore, as a result of these comparative approaches, the ways in which various forms of internal disciplinary control and normative regulation operate across institutions are illuminated. While correctional institutions are reliant on punitive action and surveillance to compel compliance, boarding schools do so by means of more refined control associated with the achievement of educational and other extracurricular activities. The comparison highlights the degree of tension between regulatory control coupled with normative influence and the different orders of that influence vis-à-vis individuals in varying institutional settings. Finally, the comparative study offers insights into the varying degrees of closure and, in relation to that, the scope of change within the boundaries of the institutions.

Halfway houses, for example, usually function as a transitional stage, permitting residents certain external contacts and even participation in rehabilitation programmes, thus demonstrating a greater phenetic boundary between the facility and the neighbouring community. In contrast, a total institution has a total separation from the outer world, and, therefore, a complete separation from the 'outsiders' is made as well. This study brings out the differences in social isolation and reintegration opportunities individuals have in various types of institutional frameworks. In short, the comparative analysis with other institutions clarifies that the total institution has a focal point in the institutional framework, and its features are particularly salient, as well as its effects on the lives of the people. This technique is how, by comparison of contrasting institutions, we can understand the boundaries and the consequences of total institutions in relation to the developed framework of institutional sociology.

Case Studies and Real-Life Examples

To explore total institutions, it is important to view them through a lens of real life to appreciate their consequences for individuals and the community as a whole. With the help of numerous case studies and real-life examples, we can analyse the intricate features of total institutions and understand about people in these institutions more profoundly.

Perhaps one case study could examine the lived experience of people serving time in correctional facilities, with particular attention to the metamorphosis of identity and changes in social relations and social power. Another useful case is the analysis of the effects of military boot camps on recruits, with regard to the ways in which they become institutionalised and the relations of power and domination involved. In addition, the analysis of the institutional field of mental health provides a powerful example of the consequences of incarceration and the construction of a personal identity. Theoretical discussions of total institutions are best understood through the prism of practical and real life, and these case studies help illustrate such concepts. With these case studies, we are able to draw attention to the definition and the many facets of total institutions and their consequences for society as a whole. These powerful case studies remind us of the range of consequences which total institutions have on individuals, as well as the extent of the relevance of Goffman's views on such institutions.

Conclusion and Transition to Frame Analysis

As we complete the study of total institutions, it is evident that the social consequences of these particular social structures are profound and go beyond simple incarceration.

By examining specific case studies and real-life examples, this module has demonstrated how total institutions can control both individuals and the identities they adopt. From prisons to boot camps, and from asylums to convents, the breadth and depth of control and dominance these systems of closure exercise is remarkable in so many aspects of humanity. The behaviour of prisoners, alongside the processes of institutionalisation and the self, showcases the powerful nature of existence in a total institution. The next element of our study focuses on the processes of 'in' and 'out' framing. Alongside what has been said about total institutions, frame analysis is another set of tools to understand social relations and their dynamics. We will revisit Goffman's idea of frames as the cognitive scaffolding used to interpret social encounters and everyday experiences. We will also consider ways in which people construct, navigate, and manipulate these frames to control their impressions and identities in everyday performative situations.

It is juxtaposing the rigidity of total institutions with the fluidity of frame analysis that helps illuminate the contours of the social life structure and agency within the social totality. This is the differentiation that encompasses the movement from the macro-level examination of total institutions to the micro-level analysis of social reality construction and negotiation. In summary, analysing total institutions enables a deeper understanding of the intricate relationship between social structure and individual agency. We have set ourselves up to apply frame analysis to the study of social life as an outcome of interaction and interpreting. We have set ourselves the task of clarifying human behaviour and experience by closing the gap between the constraining aspects of total institutions and the interpretive flexibility and domains of the frame.

***

1. **Foucault, M. (1977).** *Discipline and Punish: The Birth of the Prison.* Translated by Alan Sheridan. Pantheon Books.

While not directly citing Goffman extensively, Foucault's analysis of carceral institutions, surveillance, and disciplinary power complements and expands on Goffman's insights into institutional control. Both explore how institutions produce docile bodies and manage identity.

2. **Sykes, G. M. (1958).** *The Society of Captives: A Study of a Maximum Security Prison.* Princeton University Press.

This is a classic ethnography of prison life that closely aligns with Goffman's framework. Sykes identifies the "pains of imprisonment" and describes how total institutions strip individuals of autonomy—echoing Goffman's concept of the "mortification of self".

3. **Clemmer, D. (1940/1958).** *The Prison Community.* Christopher Publishing House (original 1940; revised 1958).

Though predating *asylums*, Clemmer's work on "prisonisation" influenced Goffman. Later scholars often read the two together to understand how total institutions foster subcultures and reshape identity.

4. **Manning, P. K. (1977).** *Police Work: The Social Organization of Policing.* MIT Press.

Applies Goffman's dramaturgical and institutional frameworks to policing, showing how quasi-total institutions (like police academies or precincts) enforce conformity and manage front-stage/back-stage behaviours.

5. **Lemert, E. M. (1967).** *Human Deviance, Social Problems, and Social Control.* Prentice-Hall.

Engages with Goffman's ideas on labelling and institutional responses to deviance, situating total institutions within broader systems of social control.

6. **Creed, G. W. (2006).** *"Total Institutions" Revisited: Processes of Internal Colonisation in Communist and Post-Communist Romania.* In The Anthropology of Power:

Empowerment and Disempowerment in Changing Structures (eds. A. Abramson & D. Theodossopoulos), pp. 103–122. Routledge.

Re-examines Goffman's model in non-Western and political contexts, showing how state socialism created totalising environments that reshaped everyday life and identity.

7. **Fine, G. A., & Manning, P. K. (2003).** *Erving Goffman*. In *The Blackwell Companion to Major Social Theorists* (ed. G. Ritzer), pp. 473–502. Blackwell Publishing.

Provides a critical overview of Goffman's contributions, including a detailed analysis of *Asylums* and the lasting impact of the total institution concept across disciplines.

8. **Hannah, M. T. (2020).** *Total Institutions and the Reproduction of Inequality: Revisiting Goffman in the Era of Mass Incarceration.* Symbolic Interaction, 43(4), 575–596. https://doi.org/10.1002/symb.492

A contemporary reassessment of Goffman's framework in light of modern carceral systems, arguing that total institutions perpetuate racial and class-based inequalities through ritualised degradation and identity suppression.

9. **Rothman, D. J. (1971).** *The Discovery of the Asylum: Social Order and Disorder in the New Republic.* Little, Brown, and Company.

Traces the historical emergence of asylums, prisons, and almshouses in 19th-century America—providing crucial background to the institutional forms Goffman later analysed.

8
Frame Analysis
Interpreting, Organising, and Making Sense

What is Frame Analysis?

The reasons for studying frames have been described as 'cognitive structures through which people "see" and "move" within their social world' with lots of 'utilities' to their understanding and use of frames as "social frames". Frame analyses suppose sociologists and social thinkers have specific and fundamental concerns about the ways people 'read' and 'make sense of' the 'events' and 'experiences' of their social environments and interactions. This is one of the few places to synthesise the most important components and ways of understanding the development and use of frame analysis within sociology. This overview is important, especially in understanding the essence of frame analysis and its social application. This understanding and appreciation is gained from the history of the approach as it has been developed as sociological and sociological thinking as its critical and core backbone understanding and appreciation of the history of the approach.

> Erving Goffman's *Frame Analysis: An Essay on the Organization of Experience* (1974) is one of his most ambitious and complex works. In it, Goffman explores how individuals interpret, organize, and make sense of their everyday experiences through **"frames"**—cognitive structures or schemata that allow people to locate, perceive, identify, and label events within their life space.
> Core Concepts of Frame Analysis:
> **Natural frameworks** (e.g., weather, illness—events not guided by human intent)

Social frameworks (e.g., rituals, games, conversations—events involving human agency)

Primary Frameworks: Basic structures that help us interpret reality. These are divided into:

Keying: The process by which activities are transformed from one frame to another (e.g., joking, make-believe, or ceremonial speech alters the "key" of an interaction).

Fabrications: Deliberate manipulations of frames (e.g., deception, theater, propaganda).

Frame Breakdowns: Moments when participants disagree on which frame applies, leading to confusion or conflict (e.g., not knowing if someone is serious or joking).

Embedding and Layering: How frames can be nested within one another (e.g., a play within a film, or a dream sequence in a story).

Goffman's frame analysis bridges micro-sociology with cognitive and linguistic dimensions of social life, influencing fields like communication studies, media theory, linguistics, and cultural sociology.

Historical Context and Development

The history of frame analysis has roots in sociological thinking and development. The history of frame analysis can claim some of its dominance from the original writings of Erving Goffman, who, in the exploration of the social world and actions of the people with their actions in daily activities and the puzzle of meaning in daily life, was the first to develop some of the cornerstones of this approach.

Goffman's study of the intricacies of human activity and social structures during the 1900s served as the basis for the formation of frame analysis. Frame analysis as a concept was developed simultaneously with a broader scope of sociological theory. It developed alongside the formation of symbolic interactionism, which considered social reality to be a construction and emphasised the functions of symbols within human behaviours, particularly during interaction. Such an intellectual climate, which started focusing on the study of micro social relations, was ripe for Goffman's innovative formulation of frame analysis. The development, or rather, the historical development of frame analysis, as with other sociological concepts, did not happen in isolation from the societal changes that came after World War II. The pattern of urbanisation, the advancement of technology, and the restructuring of social roles during this period provided new opportunities for the analysis of the intricacies of human behaviour. These changes required new frameworks for analysis, which frame analysis was able to provide in examining the construction and interpretation of experiences of people in different social situations. The evolution of frame analysis is also part of the advancement of qualitative research methods.

As scholars became fascinated by the details of personal experiences and meaning construction, seeking methods to analyse the minutiae of daily life became a priority. Researchers studied social interactions and the interpretive frames that shape their understanding in great detail. The outline of the vigorous historical context reveals a distinct cross-section of intellectual discourse, novel approaches, and evolving societal conditions in the development of frame analysis. It is a volume of social history and theory, and of the development of methods to analyse the intricacies of social life and human relations.

Conceptual Foundations

To study the analysis of frames, we start with the social encounters framed by Goffman as the beginning of a quantification of a social science. The main premise addresses the mental processes involved in learning and understanding the social 'realities' that bind each individual as a member of a specific group. The genesis of frames analysis is the corpus of sociology understood through Goffman from my perspective.

Frame analysis focuses on the sociocultural structures that, on the one hand, enable but, tragically, constrain how people make sense of, interpret, and engage in their relationships with others. Thus, Goffman illustrates how people frame their perceptions and interpretations as a function of the social order, social roles, and social expectations, and in the process, social life is socialised. Moreover, the principles of frame analysis apply to the study of social order and reality construction in different social situations. This frame of reference helps understand the different ways through which people engage in meaning co-construction during their routine social interactions. This is why frame analysis provides an understanding of the depths of interpersonal social relations and the relations between people and society. Goffman still notes the gaps and the contradictions in the social structure of life. For him, the foundation of the analysis provides a broad understanding of the gaps formed in the construction of identity and the stratification of power and communication in social frames. Goffman emphasises that social frames are important tools for interpreting, managing social impressions, and making sense of the social situations that people perceive as 'common understanding'.

The bases of frame analysis in social theory serve as a critical point of reference for understanding the intricate aspects of social relations and the embedding of people in social structures. This exegesis of frame analysis sheds light on the relations between cognition, culture, and social interaction and analyses the definitional frameworks that make sense of human behaviour and social arrangement.

Key Theoretical Constructs

The framing of social behaviour theory in frame analysis attempts a sophisticated treatment of the phenomena which govern social conduct and control individual actions. For social theory, a 'frame' is a critical concept in Goffman's theory; it is a mental construct that structures cognition and the interpretation of experience, events, and interaction in social settings. These social schemata assist people in 'thinking through' the complexities of the social world and direct their self-actions to social cues, determining their behaviour and responses to events. These theories also support the construction of the social world and social reality through interpretation and meaning. The theory of framing principles is a critical concept that explains the endorsement processes within the social definitional stream, where individuals define, interpret, and redefine the boundaries of their embedded situations.

The principles' adaptability and contextual characteristics have been elucidated through their flexible, changing application to given circumstances. Grasping how the principles of framing work together is essential in understanding how people socialise and collaboratively develop understandings in their social circles. Building on these ideas, Goffman spins the social world around the interplay of primary frameworks and keyings with more authority. As primary frameworks, these highlights, which are based on cultural and social conventions, become the first anchors of analysis in defining and understanding social encounters. They outline the shared understanding of how to act and speak in relation to and with others. Similarly, keyings explain how people work on fitting their behaviour within particular frames to project certain images and intentions. Within particular frames, behaviour is modified so that it expresses a particular desired wish. The above principles also support the study of metaframes, which are the dominant systems of society that determine how frames are created and spread in different systems of institutions. The interconnections Goffman draws between metaframes and individual frames illustrate the intricate relationship between macro- and micro-sociological phenomena.

Furthermore, the identification of key theoretical constructs provides valuable information concerning the complexity of social order through the interaction between internalised frames and external institutions. Simply put, having insight into the key theoretical constructs of frame analysis helps provide a deeper understanding of the complexity of social situations and the dynamics involved in human interaction. This paper serves as a beginning to explore the use of frame analysis in different social situations, thus demonstrating its importance in the understanding of social life and its complexities.

Use in Social Interaction

The theoretical frame has been and continues to be useful in understanding and explaining social interactions in a continuum of human activities. Its use is found in such disciplines as sociology, psychology, communication, and social anthropology, among others. By studying the dynamics of frame analysis, scholars have been able to offer explanations for the more subtle and profound interactions between people and social systems. In sociology, the use of frame analysis has helped in understanding the ways through which individuals perceive and mentally construct meanings to social situations of their daily life.

Research has been able to shed light on crafted features that govern ties, including rules, norms, and interface expectations, thanks to social framing. This crafted feature has also been described as an effective way of investigating identity, power, and social class relation issues in different contexts. In other disciplines, psychology in particular, frame analysis has been indispensable in enriching descriptors and distinctions of social behaviour. This has been done by analysis of the framing of social encounters. The analysis of social encounters has positioned psychologists to better understand the decision-making process, feelings and behaviour of individuals, as well as the controlling power of the environment on the individual. These developments have been noted in clinical psychology, social psychology, and behaviour within organisations; thus, the understanding of social phenomena framing has proven to have functional value for social change and control.

Wide understanding in frame analysis embeds the study of social phenomena such as interaction, contact, and exchange. With regard to other disciplines, the study encompassed in frame analysis is communication. This study has also been taken for much advantage in public communication by providing instruments for studying narratives, discourse, and symbols used in the field of communication on different matters. From the analysis done, it has been noted that scholars have been able to study and explain the framing of news stories, advertisements, political discourse, and even social media to glue together how the public thinks and acts.

Moreover, frame analysis has been crucial in the study of the persuasive techniques used in public communication, including the framing of social problems during public discussions. For example, anthropologists have used frame analysis to study rituals, cultural practices, and symbol systems within a society. This combination of disciplines has greatly enhanced our understanding of how meaning is created and interpreted within various cultural contexts. Through analysis of the framing of cultural events, anthropologists have been able to understand the social and symbolic aspects of rituals, ceremonies, and social customs, demonstrating the wide diversity of social systems and the intersymbolic relationships among them. The use of frame analysis in the study of social relations is diverse and is still expanding due to the impact of new research and collaborative work across different disciplines. The growing interest in the method's application for various purposes and contexts will make sure it retains its central position in the study of human social behaviour and its unparalleled significance.

Methodological Approaches

Methodological approaches of frame analysis are critical in understanding the function of frames in social interaction. This section provides insight into the complex approaches taken to explain and analyse frames in social settings. The analysis of frames often requires an integration of qualitative and quantitative techniques in framing processes. Ethnography and in-depth interviews as qualitative techniques provide the best descriptions of how people create and negotiate frames in daily communication interactions. Also, content and discourse analyses help systematically determine the existence and the impact of frames in communication and media. Such qualitative techniques assist in answering what meanings are intended and the interpretations that are associated with the frames. Quantitative approaches, such as surveys and field and laboratory experiments, help explain the extent and consequences of framed messages at a macro level. Quantitative approaches provide evidence of the existence of predictive relationships in frame analysis and alignment, as well as frame dissemination. Analyses of diverse data sets using mixed-method approaches provide a methodological opportunity to confirm findings and enrich frame analysis.

Participatory observation and fieldwork are ideal ways to enhance the researcher's understanding of the construction and performance of frames in real-world contexts and interactions among individuals, groups, and institutions. In addition, the use of photographs, videos and other forms of visual methodologies provides profound insights into the analytical aspects of framing, such as posture and other gestures. These techniques provide an innovative understanding of the nuanced frames in social life. Ethical issues, such as informed consent, privacy, and the need to work with sensitivity when researching marginalised populations, are as central to the methodological issues as the use of frame analysis. Ethical research practices such as protecting the privacy of the subjects and the reputational risks that come with such frame analysis will help build high-quality sociological insights. To summarise, the methodological approaches to frame analysis integrate various forms of qualitative and quantitative approaches, and even mixed methods, each of which adds value to unlocking the mystery of the framing processes in the diverse social contexts.

Critical Perspectives

This part focuses on analysing the critical aspects of using frame analysis as a theoretical approach. The application of frame analysis in different social contexts has triggered important debates, and scholars have pointed out many issues that arise from using frame analysis in social research.

A detractor's primary focus is the reductionist tendency of frame analysis applied to social phenomena. While social interactions are more complicated than just the constituent interactions between people engaged in a social frame, the emphasis on 'framing' rests on the frames themselves. Some critics discuss a significant deficit in the depth of interrogation regarding power relations within frame analysis. It is a concern that some frames may mitigate power relations considered in the social critique of frame analysis. This critique tends to focus on the ways frame analysis, designed to interrogate relationsin fact, quantifies power relations of dominance to expose structures of marginalisation dominantly performed. Reflexivity is also a facet of critical analysis that remains unexplored. The discussion has also addressed how frame analysis supports its own argument and the potential interrogative value derived from the research participants. The critique of reflexivity particularly is associated with the concern of the internal relations between, and among, frames, and between an individual and social frames and social structures, urging sensitivity to the triumph of reductionism. There continues, however, to be a critical discourse on the cultural and contextual reach of frame analysis, and this is particularly important. Critical discourse provides the frame to appreciate the analysis of differences in cultural and historical contexts relevant to frame analysis, particularly to frame analysis that does not critique itself on culturally determined assumptions.

This discussion seeks to develop and deepen the theoretical underpinnings of frame analysis with an expanded and culturally aware perspective. Within these critiques, it is essential to appreciate the effort put into engaging with different theoretical and methodological approaches. Scholars try to tackle the complexities and subtleties that frame analysis bypasses by incorporating intersectional approaches and interdisciplinary lenses. This reflection deepens and broadens the intellectual frames and scope of social interaction understanding. Thus, the fundamental critiques of frame analysis and the perspectives it is approached from provide an iterative examination of the theory, the methods, and the ethics of frame analysis. Accepting these critiques allows us to expand the reflexivity and flexibility of frame analysis, thereby enhancing its geographical and sociocultural relevance.

Comparative Analysis with Total Institutions

Here, we compare some aspects of frame analysis with the total institutions as defined by Erving Goffman. Goffman describes total institutions as the places where people are enclosed and controlled by the same rules and regulations that dominate all other aspects of life: prisons, asylums, and barracks.

These settings lose individuals' identities due to their strict social supervision and lack of personal freedom. On the other hand, the frame analysis focuses on the cognitive processes that construct the perception and interpretation of social situations, including the self-definition and self-positioning relative to these situations. While the two concepts have different focusses, they share a common goal of diagnosing the processes that construct and maintain social order. This procedure is how we approach the differences and similarities between the two concepts in their most critical form, covering the processes of institutionalisation and the shaping of social realities along with the order of control.

Transitions to Gender and Interaction

In the Movement to Address Gender and Interaction, the shift is from a comparative analysis of total institutions to an in-depth analysis of the social constructs of gender and their interrelationships with routine social processes. We will demonstrate the ways in which individual gender performances are tied to different interactional frames, drawing on the work of Erving Goffman, particularly his foundation on the elements of symbolic interactionism.

We start with the framework of gender as an integral element of social interaction analytics, paying attention to performative identity as well. We then investigate the internalisation of gender norms as they concretise in social life, influencing the processes of self-presentation and impression management. Using Goffman's theories on dramaturgy, we analyse the subtle micropolitical strategies of individuals in gendered situations. This includes examining the functions of symbols, gestures, and language in maintaining and challenging social gender boundaries in the interactional context. Furthermore, the integration of gender with other categories, such as race, class, and sexuality, is critically analysed to shed light on the complex interconnections in social life. Using an interdisciplinary framework, we aim to figure out how individuals navigate and contest externally imposed gendered constraints on their social interactions. We illustrate the fundamental fluidity and variability of gendered performances and the means by which people reposition and redefine interactional gendered scripts through the diverse examples and case studies we provide.

This part also looks at the consequences of gendered relationships in the institutional domains of learning and other workplaces to reveal the deeply ingrained power relations and systemic discrimination in these spaces. We go beyond the unactionable precepts of 'watching and doing nothing' to the 'working to create' inclusive and equitable relations in the interface of society. In this case, we seek to equip the readers with the insights and skills to diagnose and combat the discriminative practices of profound gender discrimination.

Each time we make the metamorphosis to gender and to interaction, this part is key to pivoting from the most basic elements of frame analysis to the most sophisticated gendered complexities of social life. It enables them to appreciate the analysis of the deeply layered construct and action of symbols and their own position in the ever-complexing drama of social life.

Final Thoughts

In this last part, we have examined some of the fundamental issues concerning the interrelation of gender and interaction with the knowledge of frame analysis as a tool to uncover some of the central issues in social life. As we close this chapter, it is important to think about the primary issues, and the lasting importance of these arguments is to move to the next step.

Gender and interaction have been an important part of studying sociology. Their intersection with frame analysis has illuminated pivotal attributes of the framings that govern our daily exchanges. This specific analysis has also made it clear that we need to recognise that social structures, rules, and power relations are all fundamental to constructing gender identity and roles within different frames.

Considering gender interaction in detail helps us appreciate the complex and multifaceted character of behaviour and the perpetuation of social phenomena. This gives us the possibility to more effectively confront the challenges of traditional views and other forms of discrimination to create more inclusive and socially equitable conditions.

Besides this, the use of frame analysis in the study of gender and interaction clarifies the dimensions that shape personal and social phenomena. It also helps to suggest possible solutions to the questions of representation, voice, and identity.

The socioeconomic factors within gendered interaction spaces require us to recognise the shortcomings and biases of the frames being used. By concentrating on the theory and practice of frame analysis, we can strive for contextualised and more inclusive interpretations of the social dynamics of gender.

This critical reflection enhances our awareness and appreciation of the diverse experiences and hardships faced by complex individuals, particularly in relation to amplifying the voices of marginalised groups. As for the rest, the analysis of gender and interaction regarding frame analysis does not only add to the understanding of the social world but also highlights the valuable contribution of sociological imagination. The productive and practical approach to the still-developing aspects of gender, empowerment, and social change within the context of sociological reflection must rest on the intersectionality and fundamental questioning of the frameworks of the paradigm. These critical reflections promote active participation in the fight against the roots of inequality to build societies characterised by diversity and social justice.

***

Levinson, S. C. (1992). *Activity Types and Language.* In P. Drew & J. Heritage (Eds.), *Talk at Work: Interaction in Institutional Settings* (pp. 66–100). Cambridge University Press.

Builds on Goffman's framing to analyse how conversational participants use "activity types" as interactional frames to coordinate meaning.

Tannen, D. (1993). *Framing in Discourse.* Oxford University Press.

This book is a foundational collection of essays that apply Goffman's frame concept to linguistics and discourse analysis. Tannen explicitly credits Goffman and extends his ideas to narrative and conversational framing.

Gamson, W. A., Croteau, D., Hoynes, W., & Sasson, T. (1992). *Media Images and the Social Construction of Reality.* Annual Review of Sociology, 18, 373–393. https://doi.org/10.1146/annurev.so.18.080192.002105

The article delves into Goffman's impact on media framing theory, making a distinction between his interactional "frames" and later journalistic or political "media frames".

Bateson, G. (1972). *Steps to an Ecology of Mind.* Chandler Publishing.

Though predating Goffman's *Frame Analysis*, Bateson's work on "metacommunication" and "play frames" directly influenced Goffman; scholars often read them together to understand the origins of framing theory.

Kendon, A. (1990). *Conducting Interaction: Patterns of Behaviour in Focused Encounters.* Cambridge University Press.

The book applies Goffman's framing to embodied interaction, demonstrating how participants use gaze, posture, and gesture to signal frame shifts, such as transitioning from casual chat to serious talk.

Benford, R. D., & Snow, D. A. (2000). *Framing Processes and Social Movements: An Overview and Assessment.* Annual Review of Sociology, 26, 611–639. https://doi.org/10.1146/annurev.soc.26.1.611

While focused on social movement theory, this review acknowledges Goffman as a precursor to framing in collective action, though it distinguishes his micro-interactional approach from strategic movement framing.

Smith, P. (2010). *Cultural Theory: An Introduction* (2nd ed.). Wiley-Blackwell.

Chapter 4 ("Dramaturgy and Interaction Ritual") includes a clear exposition of Goffman's frame analysis and its place in symbolic interactionism and cultural sociology.

Duranti, A. (2009). *The Relevance of Goffman for Ethnography.* In J. G. H. Briggs (Ed.), *Goffman: Exploring the Interaction Order* (pp. 31–58). Polity Press.

The text underscores the ways in which Goffman's concept of frames influences ethnographic techniques, particularly when examining the co-construction of situational definitions by participants.

9
Gender and Interaction
Construction and Consolidation of Gender Roles

An Overview of the Gender Dynamics

The influence of gender dynamics on self-perception and perception of others in a given social setting and society at large is quite expansive. The purpose of this chapter is to examine the complexity and multidimensionality of gender dynamics in social interactions from a historical, sociological, and psychological lens. Focusing on the construction of gender and the historical development of gender roles, this chapter attempts to explain the development of norms and expectations and the more complex aspects of the development of contemporary gender roles. What, in the last few decades, has become of more interest to scholars is the role of culture, social structure, and dominant ideology in the construction and consolidation of gender roles.

We seek to understand the social psychology of gender interaction and the correlated social behaviours of the dominant ideology. Focusing on the interdisciplinary approach in gender studies which emphasises the role of scholars and theory builders in gaining a systematic knowledge of interpersonal relations, this particular chapter seeks to explain the performance and negotiation of social interaction in the context of gender within diverse social interactions. We will highlight the sociological, anthropological, and feminist theoretical aspects of the performance of gender.

We will then analyse the dimensions of the culture of power, the social expectations, and the cultural scripts of the gendered interactions. Personal free will is delicately balanced with self-imposed rules. Civilisation and social in-

ERVING GOFFMAN: OBSERVING THE UNOB... 163

tercourse as a whole are closely woven, and the primary threads of the weave are gender. There are social norms and genders that intertwine and interlace the whole. There is the complex and the simple. Composed of various threads and social identity. All completing the whole, the second is untamed, the second is untouched. There are significant issues related to social identity that remain unexplored; the second set refers to the intersectionality of these identities. The whole is a social enclosure.

Gender is a strain that constricts movement; its pervasiveness is baffling. We try to cover its arch in space. Alongside the chapter lies social philosophy. To advance the study, there will be many theories and questions that will hinder. All will be posed first; the foundation will be the woven fabric. Gender is the centre that every student spins on. For its study, interaction is fundamental. It is a bridge towards the gender issues. This whole area is rich with gender issues. All reside in civilisation.

> While Erving Goffman did not write a single monograph exclusively on gender, his analyses of everyday interaction, impression management, and the presentation of self laid crucial groundwork for understanding gender as a performed, interactional achievement—a perspective that deeply influenced feminist theory, queer studies, and the sociology of gender.
>
> Goffman's key insights on gender appear across several works, notably:
> - The Presentation of Self in Everyday Life (1959) – on dramaturgy and performance

- Behaviour in Public Places (1963) – on gendered spatial conduct

- Gender Advertisements (1976/1979) – his most direct analysis of gendered visual codes

- Forms of Talk (1981) – on gendered speech patterns and conversational roles

In Gender Advertisements, Goffman famously identified recurring visual tropes (e.g., the "feminine touch," "ritualisation of subordination") that encode power and gender through posture, gaze, and positioning—anticipating later work on the social construction of gender.

Historical Perspectives on Gender Roles

The interaction of society as a whole is the foundation of every interaction. The commitment and accomplishments of every civilisation are influenced by gender roles. This and also the norms were meant to streamline social flows. Gender on the one side and civilisation on the other side is the social world.

For many societies, the expectations and roles of gender were rigid, each with one of a range of behaviours, deserved duties and endorsed privileges, all for one sole purpose.

Societal norms and cultural perceptions often dictated a person's social standing and access to resources, and even how the resources could be used, from the earliest times, on account of one's gender. Throughout history, many civilisations subsisting on a patriarchal system stifled women's status by imposing and solidifying male dominance and control. The consequences of such control, however, affected every aspect of life, including family, work, politics, and even religion, creating profound and lasting inequities and gaps. The ramifications of gender definition, shaped historically, still define the manner in which social interactions occur and spaces are moved through. Studying how gender roles evolved sheds light on the social interactions which are still fraught with inequality and inadequacy when concerning gender. This suggests the need to confront and dismantle restrictive and outdated norms about gender which still control and constrain social behaviour. The need to comprehend the unsophisticated thinking that still underlines social interactions about gender dynamics in the present, to bring about appropriate action, has to start from history itself. This truism still serves as a basis to encourage broader interactions that are socially considerate and equitable with respect to the underpinnings of gender roles.

Theoretical Foundations: Goffman's Contribution

As eminent a sociologist as Goffman was, his work concerning the social performance of gender and interactions was equally foundational in his sociological work.

While Goffman examines actions that people take in everyday life to construct social reality from a symbolic interactionist perspective, he also comments on gender and interaction in a way that emphasises the tactics individuals use to manage and strategically construct social contexts. 'Impression management' or 'presentation of self' focuses on the processes individuals employ in actively attempting to control how other people think and feel about them. Goffman views social life, in this sense, as a drama where people take different parts and follow gender roles. This approach allows for a more comprehensive understanding of gender and gender self-presentation, which people perform and on which people act in their daily lives. For Goffman, gender is more than just an identity; it is a performance that is constructed in social practices, norms and interaction. Goffman also comments on the dynamics of power in face-to-face interaction to illustrate how social encounters are, in many ways, encounters of gender. In focusing on micro-level interactions of social life, Goffman also emphasises the potent and fine-drawn ways in which gender is performed and sustained in social relations.

Goffman's theories have been crucial to unpacking the nuances of gender expression and its interaction with other identities such as class, race, and sexuality. His observations on the variability and situational aspects of gendering oneself use an essentialist approach and highlight the constructionist approach to gendering. In addition, Goffman's contributions lay the foundation of understanding the performatively of gender within broader social and cultural frameworks. As feminism has evolved, the scholarly works that have built on Goffman's work continue to use his theories to trace the interconnectedness of gender and social interaction. His works provide a complex approach to the intricacies of gendered social actions, social expectations, and the power relations that are intertwined in them.

Performing Gender: The Social Script

In the study of interaction, the notion of performing gender has been a pivotal concept in helping us understand how people articulate and perform their gender in social scenarios. Using Goffman's sociological imagination, this segment of the book focuses on the complexity of gender performances as social scripts that define and structure our interactions. The construction, expression and cultural dictates of gender, together with societal expectations and personal agency, blend to form a dense web of gendered actions and symbols.

The concept of performing gender revolves around 'impression management'. In this realm, people either deliberately or unconsciously alter their behaviour to adopt and 'perform' a certain gender identity. This behaviour can be expressed through the use of verbal language, body language, the wearing of certain clothes, and any other form of symbolic behaviour that conforms to the gender that is considered socially constructed. They adopt the behaviours as set out in the scripts, which, in turn, allows society to maintain and reinforce rigid gendered behaviour and the simplistic binary that underpins masculinity and femininity in social situations.

Moreover, the performance of gender takes the individual actions of people, including their interactions and social reputational systems. It is the socially constructed system of gender that enables the performance of certain behaviours to be classified as feminine or masculine, and privileges or marginalisation within gendered interactions expose social injustice. The merging of gender and performance as a complex, multi-layered dimension of social interaction includes the specific cultural, historical, and changing social contexts and movements of the times that add to the complexity of gender performance. This section attempts to understand the complex relationship of gender with the social whole, recognising the performance of gender that is beyond the binary and rigid categorisations of gender as fluid and diverse.

The social script helps us understand the complex ways in which gender is performed, contested, or bypassed in the context of everyday life.

Gendered Rituals and Encounters

The influence of gendered rituals and encounters is primary in theorising social interaction and relation. These rituals are part of universal and cultural systems, and they shape how people situate gender in context. In the study of gendered rituals, we analyse the complex array of actions, movements, and signs that construct and sustain the social order of gender. My focus will be on the gendered worlds of rituals and their meanings. These rituals automate the performance of gender, framing it in a context of behavioural and emotional programming that is obligatory for those who fall within the categories of the social binary. In all of its forms, gendered behaviour, both at the level of micro and macro rituals, is controlled and regulated ritualised behaviour with its own sophisticated systems of power. In addition, gendered encounters can serve as a useful tool for analysing power relations and social stratification. In the context of daily life or within more institutionalised environments, for example, the workplace or public sphere, gendered encounters illustrate relations of power and inequality.

While these encounters are shaped by personal actions, they are still subject to deeper systems and cultural norms regarding appropriate behaviours for each gender. Using Goffman's theory on gendered rituals and encounters helps illustrate how people 'choose' to and 'perform' gender during interpersonal exchanges. Goffman helps in clarifying how people assembling 'costumes' for their 'acts' in accordance with social norms retain the upper hand in gender performances and are also free to define their identity. On top of that, the intertwining of gender and other identity dimensions like race, ethnicity, sexuality, and social class adds more nuances to the rituals and encounters of gender. These interconnections illuminate the complexity of social encounters and interactions by revealing the necessity to understand how different social elements work together to shape people's actions, experiences, and interactions. The more scholars and researchers work on gendered rituals and encounters, the more they are left with the necessity to investigate the implications of these social phenomena on the realities people face. The more we understand the implications of gender on these social encounters, the more we will be in a position to shape inclusive policies that respond to the diverse gender interactions and expressions.

Influence of Cultural Norms on Gender Interaction

The changing interaction patterns in any society, when

looked at from the perspective of diverse cultures, have been a field of research interest in the sociology of culture. For this reason, the beliefs held by a people, whether contested or taken for granted, dictate the behaviours that are expected in society based on a socially ascribed or defined gender. To appreciate these boundaries and regions marked by the zones of cultural interaction, it is important to study the customs and traditions of a society. Boundaries go beyond roles that are considered socially acceptable; they also include gender teaching and the illustrations of man and woman, even a deeper and wider perception of cultural domination. Linked to these lines are the functions of the customs of a society that structure institutions and systems. Norms establish the social distance between individuals and regulate the permissible perceptions.

For instance, in some societies, there are different approaches between men and women. Some social systems uphold and implement structures that are otherwise more widely defined and exhibited, like the practice of gender crossing or mixing fabrics. In other cultural contexts, the feminine gender systems and structures maintain the traditional barefoot coverings worn by men as well as the skirts worn by women. Some societies define dominant cultural practices normatively and exercise them privately at a social distance. Certain divisions of work and gender, along with more seamless integrations of active cultures, highlight the dominant actions influenced by borders and self-imposed forces. Silently, societies provide a more defined concept, blurring the actions of confined systems.

By adhering to another culture and its related systems, people gain a deeper understanding of boundaries and the concept of micro-regions. In this interaction, some of the more dominant contacts fiercely control social exchanges, building thicker territories and behaviours that resonate with others. Norms from other societies and actions can create some distance, echoing more defined regions. In a dominant cultural system, individuals can express their identity within either an ascribed or undefined cultural region.

The intersection of culture and gender, along with their interactions, is multifaceted and requires precise study and understanding. Additionally, cultural traits can overlap with other social attributes such as race and ethnicity, class, and sexual orientation, thus making the gendered interactions even more complicated. Any attempt to assess the impact of cultural traits on gendered interaction requires historical, anthropological, and sociological lenses. Understanding the source of these norms and their trajectories aids in comprehending their relevance to current gendered relations. Furthermore, understanding how cultural norms support and challenge gendered normative social roles helps illuminate the prospects for social changes and developments. Understanding the impact of cultural traits on gendered interaction helps ascertain the breadth, depth, and complexity of social interactions and attempts to develop more socially and gender-inclusive constructs and relations.

Micro-Interactions and Power Dynamics

Micro interactions are fundamental elements of the social world, involving nearly every exchange, characterised by the exchange of messages and gestures, as well as the actions of each participant during daily contacts. In all these micro-interactions, the dynamics of dominance and subordination shape the social landscape.

Stratified forms of power are also tied to gender units, which people wield when navigating different levels of social systems. Goffman's methodologies can be used as a heuristic to uncover these fragile forms of power during social exchanges. The most fundamental elements of these micro-exchanges are the power and control that are exhibited, which are most readily visible through body, vocal, and geo-metrics. These social behaviours can also indicate dominant and subordinate social positions within a particular interaction. The intricately discoursed gendered relations of power can be mapped out within multiple domains and scopes of life ranging from the professional realm to the domestic sphere, which suggests a strong correlation between social control and gender. Moreover, unequal relations of power can serve to control the distribution of conversational space, as well as the allocation of recognition for participation in the dialogue. Gender can play a crucial role in shaping the social order by controlling the discourse and determining which voice receives attention. Such phenomena do not only illustrate the prevailing relations of power in society but also serve to shape and sustain the dominant constructions of gender. In addition, another aspect of the process of microsocial interactions is agency and resistance. Agency refers to the negotiated power that individuals can use to change or challenge existing social power relations and the reproduction of subordination, thereby resisting the prevailing dominant order.

Goffman's notion of impression management describes the ways in which individuals manage interactions to gain control and manipulate the power relations within them.

As we continue to examine the details of micro-interactions and power relations, it becomes increasingly clear that, far from being static, these relations are open to negotiation, contestation, and change, which capture the workings of social relations in constant flux. Analysing these power relations enables us to explore their consequences for gender equity and self-identity, as well as the reproduction of social order. These interwoven arrangements are critical for understanding the need to transform environments that normalise dominance and exclusion.

Intersectionality and the Complexity of Identity

Intersectionality is a vital tool in understanding intricate social identities in an individual's experience and in social structural arrangements, which serves as the basis of the framework for analysing self and society. First coined by Kimberlé Crenshaw, an intersectional approach to social structures interweaves social categorisations of race, gender, class, sexuality, and ability, pointing out that it is essential to examine these matrixed relations to understand how each of them works in an individual and societal context. In social relations, particularly regarding gender, understanding intersectionality is crucial for grasping the complexities that arise within these relationships.

Gender alone incorporates different identities, which will lead to complex and intricate experiences. The balance of identity gets even more complex through the imbalances that come from different intersections. The mosaic of their identities makes each person's relationship with society unique. For example, a woman of colour is likely to experience different problems than a white woman due to the intersection of racism and sexism. The same goes for a disabled person who would experience sexism much easier than a woman without a disability. By examining the intersections of identity, we can gain a deeper understanding of the diverse ways individuals engage with and experience social processes. We must analyse social order and social phenomena that sustain inequality from the perspective of intersectionality. Neglecting the intersections of identities creates a significant value gap. The focus on intersectionality in the study of inequality and the interaction of gender and social relations enables access to silenced structures and dominant ideas. It adds a value system that is appropriate to the nuances of the relationship between gender and social interaction. This perspective straightens society.

Moving on, researchers and practitioners need to add intersectionality to their analysis of gender and interaction. Adoption of this approach enhances comprehension of the intricacies of identity and allows for greater appreciation and understanding of the nuances of social relations.

Critiques of Traditional Gender Analysis in Interaction

In the past few years, the analysis of gender in interaction has faced several critiques. The primary critique of most gender analyses in social interaction is the binary approach to gender diversity and the fluidity of gender identity. Scholars provide such criticism to highlight that this oversimplified approach completely misses the intricacies of gender non-conforming individuals. Some critics argue that these gender analyses lack a genuine understanding of social relations because they fail to challenge the perpetuated power dynamics and stereotypes. Another critique is regarding the scope of the analysis, which tends to ignore the intersectional complexity of identity; race, class and sexuality are often secondary in analysis.

Moreover, there are new worries that past analyses of gender may oversimplify gender constructs, thus neglecting personal agency and self-cultivation. Scholars now advocate for frameworks that are wider and more sophisticated in appreciation of the complex and diverse features of gender. Such frameworks affirm the pluralism of identities and recognise the constitutive, fluid, and complex nature of gender as it is shaped by social exchanges. Advocates of this new, alternative angle stress that gender interactions cannot be adequately understood without taking the social, autobiographical, and geo-historical aspects of social life into consideration. In addition, they focus on the need to recognise and appreciate diverse gender self-expressions and emphasise the need to remove the silencing on self-expressions and to remove the social norms that restrain self-expressions and gender norms, particularly within the framework for the analysis of social interaction. Gender analysis of social interaction also must be responsive to the need to address deep-seated inequities, unequal distributions of power, and violence in the form of oppression that are central features of conventional analyses of gender of social interaction. By engaging with critiques of traditional gender analysis in social interaction, scholars can foster new and profound self-reflection that promotes the development of more inclusive, self-aware, and socially relevant scholarship on interpersonal relationships.

Future Directions for Gender Studies in Social Contexts

There is a need to pay more attention to gender studies within social contexts and extend beyond just adding the missing pieces.

As we look ahead, it will be necessary to foster more pluralistic and thorough research frameworks that move beyond the binary frameworks of gender. The next frontier for gender studies will include not just the impact of gender on social relations, but also the complex constituents that various identities add to these relations. One important area for inclusion in future research is the study of non-binary and trans people in gender studies. This involves understanding how social structures and expectations govern and restrict the lived experiences of people who do not meet the rigid rules of gender. Such work will not only enhance our understanding of gender in social contexts but also expand our social empathy and concern. Moreover, future work on the subject should focus more on the social relations of power within gendered interactions. More specifically, the study of the social relations of power to class, race, and gender within particular social contexts will help us better understand the processes of social inequality and the formation of the submerged population. To effectively address the systemic exclusion of individuals from full participation and agency across the gender spectrum, it is essential to better understand these processes and structures of social, economic, and political power. Still, and perhaps most importantly, future gender studies must include a more thorough integration of more diverse and complex transnational and global frameworks.

It is important to note that social norms and roles are contingent on culture and differ between societies. Cross-cultural studies help scholars better explain the complexities of gendered social behaviours and help them attain a more diverse and rich understanding of the phenomenon. There is also untapped potential in using multiple disciplines to approach gender within social contexts. Gender studies scholars stand to benefit from cooperation with psychologists, anthropologists and sociologists to develop new ways of understanding the complex relations between gender and social behaviours. Using multiple disciplines enhances the researcher's toolkit and guarantees a comprehensive and intricate study of gender relations. It is important to mention that focusing on gendered social behaviours is the first step towards a more encompassing approach to social relations. Researchers focusing on socially gendered behaviours should be careful in generalising the experiences of women and men, strive for complexity, and celebrate the multiplicity of identities. Gender studies in social contexts stand to benefit from the application of multidisciplinary intersectional frameworks that include, but are not limited to, race, class, and sexuality.

Through these determined attempts, the future of gender studies in social settings projects the possibility of fostering a world that is empathetic and celebrates the intricacies of the diversity of gender expression.

***

Primary Source:
Goffman, E. (1977). *The Arrangement Between the Sexes.* Theory and Society, 4(3), 301–331.

Goffman directly theorises gender as a structural and interactional system of "ceremonial deference" and asymmetrical rituals in this lesser-known yet essential article.

1. **West, C., & Zimmerman, D. H. (1987).** *Doing Gender. Gender & Society*, 1(2), 125–151. https://doi.org/10.1177/0891243287001002002

This landmark article explicitly builds on Goffman's interactionist framework to argue that gender is not a role one *has* but an activity one *does* in everyday interaction. It is one of the most cited extensions of Goffman's ideas in gender studies.

2. **Butler, J. (1990).** *Gender Trouble: Feminism and the Subversion of Identity.* Routledge.

Butler draws more directly from Foucault and Derrida; she acknowledges Goffman's influence on her concept of gender performativity—the idea that gender is constituted through repeated stylised acts. Goffman's dramaturgical model provides a sociological precursor to Butler's philosophical framework.

3. **Fenstermaker, S., West, C., & Zimmerman, D. H. (1991).** *Gender Inequality: New Conceptual Terrain.* In J. Lorber & S. A. Farrell (Eds.), *The Social Construction of Gender* (pp.

283–302). Sage.

Expands the "doing gender" framework by integrating Goffman's insights on accountability and audience expectations in gendered interactions across institutional settings.

4. **Kessler, S. J., & McKenna, W. (1978).** *Gender: An Ethnomethodological Approach.* University of Chicago Press.

The book utilises ethnomethodology and Goffmanian interactionism to demonstrate how individuals interpret gender in others through visual and behavioural cues, underscoring the vulnerability and ongoing effort involved in gender categorisation.

5. **Lorber, J. (1994).** *Paradoxes of Gender.* Yale University Press.

Lorber integrates Goffman's dramaturgy into her argument that gender is a **social institution** reproduced through daily performances. She explicitly credits Goffman for showing how gender is managed in face-to-face encounters.

6. **Hollander, J. A. (2002).** *Resisting Vulnerability: The Social Construction of Resilience in the Face of Rape.* Social Problems, 49(3), 293–313. https://doi.org/10.1525/sp.2002.49.3.293

Uses Goffman's concepts of impression management and stigma to analyse how women navigate gendered expectations of vulnerability and strength—demonstrating the emotional labour embedded in gender performance.

7. **Schilt, K., & Westbrook, L. (2009).** *Doing Gender, Doing Heteronormativity: "Gender Normals", Transgender People, and the Social Maintenance of Heterosexuality.* Gender & Society, 23(4), 440–464. https://doi.org/10.1177/0891243209340097

Applies and critiques the "doing gender" framework using Goffmanian concepts to examine how binary gender norms are policed in everyday interactions, especially against transgender individuals.

8. **Goode, J. (2021).** *Goffman on Gender: Interaction Order, Embodiment, and the Presentation of (Gendered) Self.* Symbolic Interaction, 44(3), 435–453. https://doi.org/10.1002/symb.534

This article provides a recent and comprehensive reassessment of Goffman's scattered yet profound contributions to gender sociology. Goode argues that Goffman's work offers a **proto-intersectional** understanding of how gender, class, and race intersect in interactional rituals.

Part III: Method, Style, and Influence

10
The Art of Observation
Social Sciences Methods and Research Techniques

Observational Techniques

Observation techniques are crucial in understanding social behaviour and interaction in any setting. Observations of subjects in natural surroundings tend to provide valuable information about people that may not be possible to obtain with alternative methods. This part discusses primary observational techniques in social research and attempts to resolve complicated issues related to performing structured observations. In social science research, observational techniques have been used for more than 40 years in observing groups, non-verbal messages, social status, and culture, to name a few. These techniques involve noting and recording behaviour, movement, and settings without any direct intervention. Custom design makes these studies complex. Any study should identify the observation sites, the behaviour to note, and the systems of observation recording. It is important to address ethical issues related to exercise, such as privacy and confidentiality. These days, more and more sophisticated devices are available. An analogue pen and paper, video recording, and increasingly sophisticated devices are available to capture and analyse observational data.

Mastering observational techniques involves understanding the context being studied while being able to step back and record behaviours without interference. Blending observational techniques with a methodological approach requires sensitivity to the studied context. This section addresses the key principles, challenges and best practices to help social scientists use observational research to develop a more profound understanding of the social phenomena being studied.

Historical Context of Observation in Social Sciences

Observation has served as a foundational basis for the social sciences, but its rich historical context has been neglected for decades. The roots of observational techniques can be traced to early anthropological studies done by scholars like Franz Boas and Bronisław Malinowski. These early ethnographers recognised the significance of observation and its application in studying culture and human behaviour. This fieldwork has changed the scientific community, as it has set the preliminaries for other observational methods. The technique has, over time, become a part of the scientific community as social sciences started evolving.

Beginning in the 20th century, researchers like Robert Park and William I. Thomas of the Chicago School of Sociology started using observation to study city life and social relations. This was the first step to concrete, data-based research—considered a major break from notions of abstract theorising. Also, Erving Goffman's work on microsociological analysis takes observation to the level of the most trivial details of ordinary social behaviour. Goffman's concept of the performer's social role drew attention to the observation process needed to uncover the symbolic meanings of behaviour. Then, the qualitative research boom of the 1950s and 1960s enhanced the centrality of observation in the social sciences. Ethnographic, grounded theory, and naturalistic enquiries claimed observation to be a pivotal element of comprehensive, context-sensitive research. Other social researchers incorporated video, field notes, and observation schedules to capture the intricacies of social life. Outside academic circles, research across psychology, communication, and even criminology drew on the results of observation. Technology has made it possible for researchers to use new methods like virtual ethnography and digital observation in observational research.

These developments stress the importance of observational techniques staying relevant even while the social sciences shift and change. Looking at this history, one can see that observation has had and continues to have a major impact on the social sciences while also creating new ideas, new methods, and stimulating new collaborations outside the area, which also underlines the importance of social science in understanding people and society in all of their attempts.

Methods of Observational Research

As a fundamental area of social science, observational research has a broad range of methods that aim to systematically capture and make sense of people's actions and interactions in their natural surroundings. The selection of an observational method rests on the fundamental research question, the context of the research problem, and the ethical boundaries of the study. Ethnography is one of the qualitative methods that requires long-term and, in some cases, total immersion within a cultural set. This method enables in-depth understanding of social phenomena, but it requires one to be there and participate in the phenomenon of research. In contrast, rigid observational research employs coding schemes and systematic methods to analyse and evaluate behaviour. This method generates evidence and data that are both reliable and valid, allowing for easy comparison across studies and manipulation in other forms of research. Moreover, one of the most common methods in ethnography, participant observation, allows the observer to interact with the group under study. This engagement provides valuable information but also raises concerns about the objectivity of the researcher.

In non-participant observation, the researcher stays more distant and on the fringes rather than actively participating, which helps in recording data from a more neutral and balanced position. Despite these distinctions, both observation and participant types offer fundamental differences and benefits that influence the conduct of research. Overt observation is a form of observation in which the researcher aims to communicate with the subjects he or she intends to study, which allows for greater coordination but can also change the natural flow of actions and responses. Covert observation means the researcher hides the research purpose from subjects, decreasing reactivity but raising ethical concerns about lacking explicit consent. Besides the two basic types of observation, there are also other techniques that specialise in collecting data unobtrusively, which include event and time sampling. Event sampling is a method that involves recording certain target behaviours during specific time intervals. Time sampling is a method used to observe and record behaviours during designated time intervals. Unobtrusive observation methods that allow subjects to act without the researcher's direct awareness cause much less reactivity than other observation techniques. There must be careful planning in the choice of techniques and methods in the context of the research being undertaken to ensure that they are appropriate and that their strengths and weaknesses are balanced.

Next, there is a choice that is more contextualised and situation-driven, which takes into account the greater planning commitment, research aims, and the need for clear ethical boundaries.

Furthermore, the exceptional application of these methods requires extensive training, focus, and dedication to ethical behaviour to uphold the observation's purpose and authenticity.

Ethics in Fieldwork

Ethics are the most sensitive topics in any type of observational research, and especially in fieldwork, which requires personal interactions with people and communities. Researchers are obliged to adopt ethical practices to protect their subjects and the research itself. In the case of fieldwork, ethical practices include, but are not limited to, informed consent, which entails telling the subject the reason for the research, what it entails, and any possible outcomes associated with it. This covers the anonymity and privacy of subjects, especially in delicate and easy-to-exploit cases. Researchers must also be aware of the power structure in which the observer has more authority than the observed and work to prevent injury or exploitation. In addition, ethical fieldwork must ensure that the worldview of the observed subjects is not violated and any form of modification of their accounts, which is an ethical fieldwork lie, is avoided.

Additionally, researchers must consider the potential consequences of their work on the people and communities involved in the study, as well as how their conclusions may impact both the advancement of understanding and the responsible, positive use of knowledge. When diverging interests arise, ethical practice requires openness about the issues and any biases or preconceptions. Ethics also requires proper respect for culture and the relationship between fieldwork and the community. This means that researchers have a responsibility to ensure community engagement, involving the community in all stages of the research process to foster collaboration and trust.

The deliberate use of technology in research observation emphasises ethical issues concerning the use of ethical recording instruments and the methods of capturing information. There is the ethical issue of theft concerning secrecy, where it is necessary to obtain the legal permissions to protect the data and the data protection regulations that are appropriate for the ethical rule of restraint to be demonstrated. The ethical responsibilities associated with fieldwork serve as the foundation for the research described in this paper, which emphasises social responsibility, asserts the importance of ethics in observation, and underscores the necessity of respecting the dignity and rights of the individuals involved in the research.

The Role of the Observer: Subjectivity and Objectivity

In social science research, especially in the case of fieldwork, the fundamental issue concerning the 'stance' of the observer is to what degree does the close perception of the phenomena in the field give rise to and, therefore, is influenced by 'personal theories'? In this section, the focus is on the complex relations between subjective and objective in the analysis and synthesis of observational research and the confrontation of the researchers with their own subjective vision and unconcealed 'blind spots'.

The participant observer's role represents, in a paradoxical manner, both subjective and objective components. It is a well-known fact that striving for objectivity is one of the fundamental components of a scientific attitude; however, one must also accept the fact that total subjective indifference might be impossible to attain. Every observer approaches the field with their own unique collection of subjective experiences, beliefs, and culture, all of which shape their understanding and decisions. The recognition and control of inherent subjectivity is crucial to preserve the dignity of observational research. The gravamen of the issue regarding subjectivity and objectivity concerns the position of the researchers. Reflexivity is one of the crucial traits of an observer; they listen to their own subjectivity. It focuses on the ways in which personal biases shape the collection, analysis, and interpretation of data. Researchers are encouraged to practice reflexivity; that is, to repeatedly question their beliefs and examine the role their own assumptions and beliefs play in the entire research process. An observer, who is intended to be in an objective position, experiences subjectivity as an active and conscious participant in research.

Additionally, there are profound philosophical questions concerning the nature of reality that relate to the subjective and objective dichotomy. This situation leads to fundamental questions regarding the possibility of objectivity and the problem of an accepted, authoritative, neutral observer.

This theory of philosophy highlights how complex and difficult it is to untangle the subjective and the objective in some kinds of observational research, and aims to go beyond just the methodology. Here, it is important to develop strong and robust methodological approaches to limit the impact of bias and subjectivity in the recorded observations. Having more than one observer can provide more views and lessen individual subjectivity and bias. Additionally, more standardised training protocols for dual observers help in the reliability and validity of the research observation data and the results of the observations and assist in increasing the objectives of the observer. The research involves a nuanced and complex conflict between subjective and objective perspectives. The observations may lack some parts, and some of the concepts may be more important than others, which indeed requires bias and subjectivity when it comes to the objectives that the observations frame.

Observation Tools and technology

The use of observation research has become more technologically advanced. Modern observation has 'awoken' the use of video cameras, audio recorders, and even body-worn sensors as digital secondary storage. The digital secondary storage devices, fundamentally, augment the quality and quantity of the observation data and even fuel the use of uploaded video and audio files in the analysis. The addition of integrated GPS and digital mapping spatialises the social dynamics of interaction's context and the geospatial elements that structure and even influence behaviour. Also, the emergence of sophisticated data analytics and software programmes has enabled researchers to 'mass process' data, capturing so many intricate details which were almost lost earlier, simplifying the sophisticated pattern observations. Observational research has, more and more, become rigid and broad in the study of correlations by insightful conclusions.

It is crucial, however, that technological advances in observational research bring up ethical considerations and even ethical challenges. In research, ethics is at the forefront. Consider the ethical implications of a potential breach of privacy, a lack of data security, or a breach of observant research ethics. In addition, the primary focus of research work is the technological aspect of it. It requires meticulous attention to detail, reflexivity, and advanced skills in observation and reflexology.

Case Studies: Successful Observational Analyses

Case studies belonging to the social science discipline, especially those in the social sciences, are immensely advantageous in gaining an understanding of the phenomena under study. With the aid of social research, phenomena can be broken down into units, which may then be examined in detail to ascertain their wider significance. The detail and context of observational case studies significantly enhance the social picture.

Analysing different social contexts using keen observation to construct intricate narratives about social realities makes up the focus of individual case studies.

Case Study 1: Ethnographic Study of Urban Public Spaces. One of the major innovations of this study is the focus on the observation and recording of activities in city public areas: parks, plazas, and streets. Using the methods of controlled observation, the investigator was able to describe the social norms, implicit rules, and "hidden" behavioural regulations in operation. The results obtained showed not simply how the people acted, but how order and social control were constructed and maintained in the pluralistic city.

Case Study 2: Behavioural Observation in Organisational Settings. In this case study, the researcher undertook to study the employees in diverse organisational settings, from white-collar corporate offices to blue-collar factories, to understand the complex relationships and interactions that characterise a workplace. The results of this study illustrate how the researcher was able to identify important patterns of organisational decision-making, structure, governance, and control by observing controlled social activities. These findings show how organisational behaviour is influenced by prevailing organisational cultures, structures, leadership, and group norms.

Case Study 3: Analysis of Non-verbal Communication. This study focused on the observation of the interpersonal interactions in forms and contexts that were bounded with socially accepted communication.

Analysis of speech can reveal gestures, facial expressions, and posture, which can lead to the understanding of how people articulate and communicate thoughts, feelings, and ideas. Such research deepens understanding of non-verbal communication and serves as a valuable resource for professionals within the psychology, counselling, and dispute resolution fields.

It is clear from these remarkable case studies, however, that the primary output of such research is documentation of human behaviour and social systems. These case studies, which focus on specific instances of observational research, reveal how memory can capture the sensitive details of social relations. They demonstrate how crucial these records are for deepening knowledge of the social system.

Challenges Faced During Observation

Like all forms of research, observation has its specific benefits as well as a unique collection of drawbacks that any investigator is obliged to confront. The observation of behaviour in people, and especially in groups, has been the source of the greatest number of difficulties. The primary concern when assessing behaviour in the second step of the process is reactivity—the tendency for people to spontaneously change their behaviour when they know they are being watched. When such change occurs, the data being collected is of minimal or no value. The data has been totally compromised. Blending in with the surroundings or making suspicious observations are the two main techniques that have proved useful in trying to avoid reactivity.

Also, maintaining an objective stance while subjectively interpreting behaviour is difficult. The observer's viewpoints and biases can and will interfere with the data collection, which requires constant awareness and consideration of other positions. There are also practical challenges that arise with the ethical part of the observation. The problem of studying sensitive interactions without causing a breach in privacy and observing the subject without causing any harm is difficult. Maintaining ethical responsibility while achieving rich and vivid observations is a crucial and challenging aspect of observational research. Moreover, the challenges of setting unrealistic goals through uninterrupted observation, due to the conditions of the observation of nature, are a situational criterion for practical consideration. Drawing sufficient data, predicting the expected reactions, and organising seamless access and flow to the desired place for probe observation in a real-time responsive condition is elaborate. Additionally, the deciphering and constructing of the observational data are complex actions that clusters of behaviours and interactions are supposed to initiate. It will take time, and the researcher will have to deal with the actions that are being coded with an expression and an utterance. Reasoned and unreasoned gestures that are complex will also have to be taken into account. The researcher will wrestle to capture the values that are singular to the observed phenomena.

Integrating Observational Data with Other Methods

In recent times, innovations in technology have placed challenging demands on the art of observation. The use of digital communication and surveillance technology raises critical ethical dilemmas, including the blurring of privacy lines. Researchers are still in the intellectual and practical stages of addressing these ethical concerns and the realities of technology to refine their observation skills.

Observational studies often lack critical thinking and refinement, leading to multidisciplinary errors. In attempting to solve these dilemmas, researchers often address the blunders, which helps reduce laxity and contributes to enhancing the value and breadth of social science knowledge.

Observational data is a vital part of working on thorough and multi-layered social science studies. The qualitative data a researcher obtains from observation is important, but it is not the only source they should rely on. Other data sources such as multi-layered qualitative and quantitative data, surveys, interviews, or archives would considerably help strengthen the research. In this part, we shall discuss the issues of combining observational methods with the other techniques for social research.

A triangulation approach involves assessing and corroborating various findings from different data sources. This method improves overall credibility and supports more comprehensive conclusions. For instance, integrating observational data and interview responses enhances facial recognition algorithms by verifying and corroborating different data sources' insights. Connecting data through the fusion of illusory contours and features reduces potential biases that may arise from relying on a single data source. Thus, the more data types incorporated, the more the research credibility increases. Integrating data sources from observational research, especially from record-keeping systems, emphasises the iterative nature of the research cycle. While a portion of the data is derived from reports, it is common and expected for researchers to discover certain behavioural and organisational results that can be sufficiently analysed from a quantitative perspective. This cycle of constructing and deconstructing the research question enhances the scope and range while simultaneously refining the research question. Researchers often integrate observational data with data from copy-text materials to enhance their understanding of the reviewed behaviour and societal workings.

Through the use of historical documents and other hands-on data, researchers can interpret and uncover hidden contexts, trends, and cultural transformations while understanding the details of the case. This inclusion of different types of data adds richness to the social practices and structures that have been observed over time. Each new technique adds a layer and builds upon the temporality of the frameworks used in prior observations. The ethics framework surrounding the use of data and other techniques is also crucial. It is essential that the data that converges from different techniques is compliant with the ethical boundaries of each technique and the approaches taken, including the protection of the participants. Conducting these techniques ethically enhances the study's credibility and demonstrates consideration for the subjects' privacy.

In short, integrating a wide array of data techniques enables researchers to triangulate and iteratively reconstruct a thick description that advances the discipline. The data merger, along with the derived ethical principles, adds to the depth of understanding and the persuasive power of the analysis, reflecting on the social phenomena being addressed.

Concluding Insights and Implications

Other than the analysis, the use of other techniques leads to the expansion and new insights on social science.

Utilising observational data along with quantitative and qualitative approaches allows researchers to gain a holistic view of social phenomena. First, triangulation of data from various sources enables a more sophisticated and detailed analysis, reducing the drawbacks of each method used independently. Through this integration, researchers can cross-validate findings, determine correlations, and deepen their interpretations. Furthermore, the convergence of methods helps in cross-checking results, thereby improving the validity and reliability of the findings. In observational research, a convergence of methods provides social interactions, behaviours, and surroundings from multiple angles, which allows researchers to form a more complete representation of the phenomenon under investigation. Such improved representation allows researchers to construct more robust theoretical models and frameworks, thereby enhancing the understanding of intricate social interactions. In addition, the integration of observational data into broader designs enables the analysis of causation and the investigation of mechanisms behind phenomena. Incorporating observational information into experimental and survey data enables researchers to delineate the pathways, resultant structures, and mediating variables involved in social phenomena. This approach enhances theorisation and provides evidence for practical social interventions and policy development by pinpointing crucial areas that facilitate social improvement.

Disciplinary boundaries rejoice in the integration of observational data with other techniques, as they promote the nurturing of new ideas as well as new ways of thinking. They stimulate the development of innovative and new paradigms of research. Furthermore, the combination of observational data analysis with various other techniques has the potential to expand the limits of research. The combination of techniques provides sufficient contextualised data to support the practices of various other professions. Research techniques provide ample data that can impact healthcare, education, management, and public policy. Such data will allow for better decision-making, enhanced performance and service delivery, and the resolution of different social issues. Research data guides strategic thinking and fosters positive social change by bridging the gap between theory and practice. Embracing integrated methodologies boosts decision-making and the development of policy systems. Strategies built from combined methodologies will address and respond to social issues more accurately. Ultimately, research methodologies that are cross-disciplinary serve as the most valuable tool that a social scientist can possess. To address the intricate social issues, embrace various perspectives of developed social practices. More social practices will be enhanced with the more developed ways of approaching new perspectives and theories from which the practices themselves are built. Integrative and interdisciplinary thinking will enhance the quality of the system. The data brought to the attention of researchers from social behaviour and system thinking can be calculated as unified and certain proof of the capability that the systemised and blended knowledge possesses.

***

Becker, H. S. (1998). *Tricks of the Trade: How to Think about Your Research While You're Doing It.* University of Chicago Press.

Becker, a student of Goffman, offers pragmatic, insightful advice on observational fieldwork, including how to notice what others overlook and how to turn observations into sociological arguments.

1. **Emerson, R. M., Fretz, R. I., & Shaw, L. L. (2011).** *Writing Ethnographic Fieldnotes* (2nd ed.). University of Chicago Press.

This is a cornerstone text for learning how to conduct and document participant observation. It details the process of entering field sites, building rapport, taking field notes, and analysing observational data through a Goffmanian/interactionist lens.

2. **Whyte, W. F. (1943/1993).** *Street Corner Society: The Social Structure of an Italian Slum* (4th ed.). University of Chicago Press.

This classic ethnography pioneered long-term participant observation in urban sociology. Whyte's methodological appendix (added in later editions) offers invaluable reflections on the ethics, challenges, and techniques of immersive observation.

3. **Atkinson, P., Coffey, A., Delamont, S., Lofland, J., & Lofland, L. (Eds.). (2007).** *Handbook of Ethnography.* Sage Publications.

The Handbook of Ethnography includes multiple chapters on observational methods, which include debates about objectivity, reflexivity, and the role of the observer. Particularly useful are chapters by Lofland & Lofland on field roles and by Delamont on ethnographic fieldwork.

4. **DeWalt, K. M., & DeWalt, B. R. (2011).** *Participant Observation: A Guide for Fieldworkers* (2nd ed.). AltaMira Press.

This practical, step-by-step guide covers everything from gaining access to recording data, managing observer roles, and ensuring ethical standards. Widely used in anthropology and applied social research.

5. **Lofland, J., Snow, D. A., Anderson, L., & Copeland, L. H. (2006).** *Analysing Social Settings: A Guide to Qualitative Observation and Analysis* (4th ed.). Wadsworth.

The book concentrates on conducting systematic observations within natural environments. Introduces frameworks for coding behaviour, mapping social spaces, and moving from raw observation to theoretical insight—ideal for urban sociology and organisational studies.

6. **Garfinkel, H. (1967).** *Studies in Ethnomethodology*. Prentice-Hall.

While not a methods manual per se, Garfinkel's work revolutionised how social scientists observe the **taken-for-granted rules** of social interaction. His "breaching experiments" demonstrate how observation can reveal the hidden structures of everyday life.

7. **Hammersley, M., & Atkinson, P. (2007).** *Ethnography: Principles in Practice* (3rd ed.). Routledge.

Offers a balanced discussion of observation within broader ethnographic practice. Addresses issues of validity, bias, note-taking, and the relationship between observation and theory-building.

8. **Pink, S. (2015).** *Doing Sensory Ethnography* (2nd ed.). Sage Publications.

The book broadens the scope of traditional observation by incorporating sensory dimensions such as sight, sound, smell, and touch. This approach reflects contemporary shifts towards multimodal and embodied observation in digital and visual ethnography.

11
Writing Social Life
The Social Scientist's Craft and Rigour

The Foundations of Interpersonal Engagement

Social life is a complex structure formed around the interactions, relations, and experiences of people in the same community. Social life is defined beyond people's interactions. It is a dynamic pattern on which human activities are etched, representing the human experience. Every social contact and every society results from complex, heterogeneous factors that interact and intertwine to reflect the immense and rich diversity of human civilisation. As the building blocks of the social structure, the basic and interconnected aspects of social life are a sense of belonging, identity, and communal sense. People maintain their interactions and relationships on these cornerstones.

The feeling of belongingness, a primary aspect of social life, represents a broad and intrinsic human desire to connect with others and create a community. It is this yearning that urges people to affiliate with others, develop social contact, and engage in cooperative activities to promote social togetherness. Furthermore, the identity construction process within social life also encompasses social, cultural, and contextual factors.

A mix of how individual persons see themselves and the social expectations from others helps shape their identity, creating a complex understanding of who they are and how they relate to others. In addition, the social aspect of life is the perpetual co-creation of meaning; still, the story is told and retold based on common ideologies, customs, and social practices. During social interactions, people come together and, as a group, create and emphasise the meaning of the symbols, behaviours, and actions, as well as the customs and rituals to which they assign social and cultural importance. This process takes place, engrains a social consciousness that spans across society, and enriches the experiences of a society as a whole. Furthermore, some of the most apparent aspects of social life are relationships of power, social hierarchy, and social stratification. These relationships help explain how resources, valued opportunities, and social privileges are divided, which often sets the boundaries for personal freedom and individual choice. Order, social roles, social control, social norms, and social structures in society develop and act as the basic rules and guides that people accept, keep, and update.

In sum, social life is rooted in the concepts of social maturation and social structures; it encompasses the entirety of society's existence and interactions, which together form the cohesive elements of togetherness, identity, meaning, and social circulations. Understanding these complexities helps us untangle social life and appreciate the intrinsic importance of these interwoven networks for our shared humanity.

Methods of Ethnographic Writing

As a unique form of scholarship, ethnographic writing differs from other types, as it incorporates both art and academic work. Unlike a 'read the world' book, prose ethnography provides other access points to a culture, and, as such, it is meant to be an invitation to look from different vantage points. This section on 'Methods of ethnographic writing' will focus on features of ethnographic writing approaches rather than constructivist approaches, as these approaches articulate and strengthen the exposition of social realities.

Writing about the social world is inelastic. More than one ethnographic strategy or ethnographic drawing may be employed. It is as if tailor-made for a particular instance; the core of ethnographic writing and creativity is in observation. This is more than just recording what one sees, but immersion into a world to perceive the nuances of social life. Ranging from 'being in' a particular milieu to composing vibrant ethnographic accounts, the writer might be called to characterise social structures, social types, social actions, customs, social events, and manners, or das Sitte, as well as 'calming' these structures and types of actions of the 'I' and other social actors, 'sitting' in social behavioural 'captures'.

Ethnographers are storytellers who metaphorically decipher social phenomena, translate, and artistically compose slosh to systems. These recursive and inter-seriation systems are social rituals and conversational analytic structures. Ethnographic observation is a skilful craft, with definitional boundaries trimmed and textured and patterned with textured 'open' boundaries. Above all, as writing about self is 'reflexive ethnography', the ethnographic account is more than a mental act of writing about; it should be, as Goffman (1974) describes, a performance ethnography, which is about presence.

Such self-reflectiveness assures honesty and clarity when dealing with the intricacies of social life. It's one thing to internalise one's biases and self-distance from the issue under study, and another to truly internalise and empathise with the issue being presented and then truly try to inclusively represent multiple perspectives of the issue at hand. An important part of ethnographic writing is spending time nurturing the ability to tell stories so that there is an emotional and rational engagement from the audience. The ability to tell a story is much more than the ability to report what has been found – it is to construct an experience that the audience feels they are participants in the social phenomenon being illustrated. Ethnographic writing not only tries to connect with readers but also aims to give them a deeper, more colourful experience by using elements like structure, development, and theme, which are key parts of literature. Additionally, ethics are very important in ethnographic writing and are more critical than other issues because they focus on key concerns like how people are represented, getting permission, and keeping information private. Ethnographic writing must prioritise the freedom and privacy of the people being studied; without this, ethical and philosophical understanding suffers. There is a strict need for a reasonable balance between ethical thinking and the rules of research and empathy. Finally, the boundaries of disciplines are crossed in ethnography not for the sake of crossing them but so that the anthropological knowledge is not irretrievably lost amid the literary art.

Narrative Craft and Scholarly Rigour

The foundation is built on the instruments and methodologies corresponding to this component, which addresses the creation of rich, ethically responsible social life narratives, including compelling story essences.

The intersection of narrative and doctoral dissertation must be a finely tuned balance when it comes to writing an ethnography. Adding narrative elements through creative techniques within the realm of ethnography is vital for the audience's emotional and intellectual engagement. Ethnographers must exercise narrative and emotional control, describing social life with ethnographic evidence that is accurate and meticulously vetted. Both must be present.

Among the literary techniques for ethnographic writing, ethnographers must use narrative techniques and creative control. This encompasses engaging prose, emotional and thought-provoking stories, and artfully woven stories that mirror and capture various social lives and cultures. The narrative technique permits the authors, who use ethnography, to communicate the day-to-day life of a particular set of people and communities to an audience that lacks this type of social engagement. Ethnographic work, or a collection of narratives that incorporate an ethnographic style, must also maintain control of the storytelling and the accurate representation. This is done with framed and definition-based context within the narrative. Ethnographers' scholarly engagements require them to understand and write about the discipline's cutting edge, ensuring that they advance scholarly work through their ethnography. One of the major areas of conflict is in merging the poem and the academic work. Narratives that focus on the "whats and whys" of social life are essential; they, however, should not replace the data's attention in its interrogation and interpretation. In fact, ethnographic writing should embody the concept of equilibration. Ethnography as a science should not over-glorify dancer-like patterns of science. The 'narrative' should meet the empirical as pointed and accurate. Narratives, themselves, need to grapple with ethical folds about the social lives they are trying to portray. Concern about the privacy and dignity of research subjects and the studied society is the primary justification for 'responsible' storytelling. Storytelling, when properly handled, is one way of making sure that narrated lives and experiences, together with the respondents, return home safely in a meaningful and ethical manner. Ethnographers, as writers, should seek and focus on interdisciplinary engagements, seeing the rest of the work as the finishing line. The line woven in the primary and creative concepts together is the 'woven' line. Careful embroidery on the many layers of ethical narrative flow, each with its own boundary, needs to be prism-like. It is this layered complexity that determines the storytelling that matters most. Ethnographers' concern level, WEAVING, adds depth and added beauty to the woven frame.

The figures of social life produced by ethnographers can be narrative and artistic, but they remain academically rigorous and appeal to scholarly and non-scholarly readers alike.

Conveying Social Context

Providing social contexts in ethnography is an intricate task. It narrates how the larger systems and culture shape individuals and their personal lives. It captures the systems of social relations, behaviours, and the web of interaction within social settings of various systems. Understanding the socio-political, historic, and cultural underpinnings of the phenomena under study is crucial for conveying social context. This means that there must be adequate fieldwork and research to understand how different elements come together in the community or group being studied. Such context aids in constructing the foundation for analysing the behaviours, customs, and relationships discussed in ethnographic writings. Ethnographic writing must focus on behaviours, customs, and interactions that are dominant and vital. It also simplifies clarifying the different, and sometimes contrasting, aspects of social life.

This study proceeds to investigating the repercussions of economic inequality on the social relations of a given community, or the manner in which culture and systems of beliefs shape the practices and the narratives of the daily lives of its members. In making such connections, ethnographic writers craft stories that transcend the narratives of the individuals and members to demonstrate the intricate social tapestry in which they exist. The depiction of communities and individuals in the social context raises ethical concerns, necessitating the resolution of representational issues. The obligations to be truthful and responsible in accounts of social life lie beneath the need to be ethical, and these accounts should be free of biases and stereotypes. One's positionality in such accounts also matters, and attending to one's biases is necessary, which in this case leads to reflexive forms of writing that demonstrate the active presence of the author in the construction of the story. The writer's foremost goal ought to be to construct a dominant impression where the detailed and clear images vividly crystallise the different aspects of a given social context. The author must employ language that vividly depicts the social situation, encompassing its context and the relationships surrounding it. The ethnographer, wanting to immerse the reader in the social world they studied, must capture the feelings, sounds, and details of the social situation so that the reader can truly understand the social realities being described.

As a form of conveying social context, ethnographic writing can do much more than simply observe and record reality. It can also do much more than observe and record and serve to engender empathy, understanding, and critical thought about the complexities of societies.

Balancing Objectivity and Subjectivity

In ethnographic writing, the integration of objectivity and subjectivity is one of the more challenging prisms and requires a nuanced understanding of the social context described as well as of the ethnographer. Subjective and objective in ethnographic writing do not cancel each other; rather, it is the paradox of the ethnographer's practised imagination tethered to his rhetoric. Ethnographic writing focuses on the social elements and layering those elements concurrently devoid of bias. Not thinking of the subject in distorting narratives, illustrating the subject as a social phenomenon makes ethnographic writing objective, enabling the reader to come up with their own impressions of the subject as described with the texts. Ethnographic writing can be devoid of prejudice and bias, yet as rigid as the researcher wills. In documenting information surrounding the subject, the more incorporated multiple perspectives of the single subject in his text, the more nuanced and richer the subject gets. Subjectivity is not the core of the ethnographic narrative: it resides with the ethnographer and how they construct their ethnographic narrative.

Adding subjectivity enhances narratives by illustrating how emotionally and intellectually invested within a field a researcher is and strengthening the reader's connection to the topic. Striking a proper balance is the cornerstone of excellent ethnographic writing. It merges objective accounts of social phenomena with subjective analyses of the researcher's feelings and experiences. Such integration enables a fuller account of social life that combines factual information with the researcher's empathetic involvement with the studied people and communities.

Achieving this balance requires the writer to scrutinise their assumptions and biases, analyse the power relations that exist within the research, and hear the voices of the studied community. Reflexive techniques, including journaling and continuous self-scrutiny, can assist in sorting out the balance between subjectivity and objectivity in ethnographic writing.

In addition, embracing reflexivity helps the writer understand their position and how it shapes the overall research outcome. The goal is to develop a thorough and responsible account of social life. Finding a balance between being objective and subjective allows ethnographic writing to effectively describe the complicated aspects of human life while also meeting the required academic standards and ethical responsibilities of social research.

Voices and Perspectives

When studying aspects of social life, having various voices

and perspectives is critical for understanding and appreciating the intricacies of social life. The various points of understanding and experiences that different people bring to the social situation enrich its context. Therefore, when addressing social life, it is essential to listen to, understand, and incorporate various voices to achieve a more detailed and holistic understanding of social life. In any social situation, it is essential to move beyond a single perspective that dominates the discourse to enhance the representation of the community or society and truly capture the essence of social life. This, in turn, shows a deeper understanding of the community or society. Exploring a wide range of perspectives helps explain the complexities surrounding human behaviour and relationships within social structures. Every social being contributes to our understanding of social life. It is, therefore, the obligation of every person or social being to admit that the more voices incorporated in the argument, the better the story. This helps the argument go beyond the superficial understanding and embrace the real-life experiences of people and society.

Furthermore, engaging with varied perspectives fosters empathy and an understanding of connectedness, which resonates deeply with the readers. The intricate balancing act of navigating the multitude of voices and perspectives involves a tightrope walk between authenticity and ethical representation. The authenticity of each voice and ethical representation, especially how sensitive or personal matters are portrayed, are equally important. The portrayal of lived experiences from multiple perspectives must not violate ethical standards. Respect, dignity, and the true representation of the essence of the storytellers must all be maintained. Furthermore, the representation of the differing voices and perspectives is not an end in itself. It creates a space for dialogue and reflection. The readers are invited to engage with the narrative that is woven with a multitude of voices. The narrative, in turn, sets the stage for reflection, not just about themselves, but a fundamental re-examination of the social order. The readers, and themselves in particular, are expected to engage in a purposeful confrontation of the majority of their biases, preconceptions, and assumptions. It was an invitation that sought the re-examination of their intellectual and emotional registers. Ultimately, the intermingled perspectives and voices are necessary for a true and powerful telling of stories of social life.

To accept this difference means highlighting other parts of social life that clarify the complicated relationship between the observer and what is being observed in social science, and by doing this, it provides the reader with a deep and rich understanding of humanity to explore.

Capturing Phenomenology

This writing, describing the complexity of accompanying the lived experience in ethnography, concerns itself with the challenge of writing, living, and thinking 'ethnographically'. This challenge rests on the degree of knowledge, emotional depth, and sensitivity that the ethnographer possesses. For social ethnography, the focus is on the nexus of individuals within a particular social setting. The fundamental challenge is how to document these experiences faithfully in a way that is accurate and does not violate the traditions of ethnography. This is why it is critical to deepen the ethnographic imagination of the studied individuals, which is activated through the practice of doing ethnography. This engagement requires immersing oneself in the culture, customs, and daily lives of the people to cultivate an ethnographic understanding that accurately reflects their lived realities.

An unbiased representation of lived experience entails a focus on the dignity and personhood of the subject. Ethnographers have a responsibility to depict the people under study in their narratives without bias, stereotypes, or any other form of exploitation. This not only entails 'thinking and engaging with one's bias' but also soliciting the people being portrayed in order to 'have a voice' about how they are perceived. In addition, what seems to be ethical about a representation of a lived experience revolves around the issues of informed consent, confidentiality, and the right to be anonymous. Ethnographers are under pressure to interpret the beauty and trouble of life, and this means walking a thorny pathway of wanting to be truthful without compromising the privacy and dignity of the people under study. This balance can only be reached by carefully managing how information is shared and ensuring ethical standards in any form of representation. It is equally important to emphasise the capacity of lived experience narratives to bring change, especially in the hands of those perceived to be lower. Ethnographers have the responsibility of tracing the narratives of such people to fill the gaps in the historical record of those who have been oppressed, and in the process illuminating the complex diversity and strength of the human condition.

Including the lived experiences of people from different walks of life can help ethnographic writing foster a greater understanding of compassion for the shared aspects of our humanity.

Ethical Depiction

As ethnographers seek to record the social world, the ethics of life writing become critical. Conducting ethnography, particularly when writing about people and communities, requires a great deal of care and utmost concern for accurately telling their life stories. Ethnographers face numerous ethical issues and must find a balance between representing social life and protecting the privacy and dignity of the subjects. The ethical issue of informed consent is critical. Ethnographic researchers must obtain clear permission from the subjects to use their life accounts, for there are stories that have far-reaching ramifications for the subjects. There is also the ethical issue of anonymity, confidentiality, and stigmatised subjects in a life that must be taken very seriously. Special procedures for data anonymisation and subject identity protection are necessary. There are also ethical concerns regarding the balance of power in representation that require thorough examination.

Ethnographers must deeply reflect on their own social locations, as well as the privilege and bias they bring to their ethnographies, since these factors can distort their understanding of social realities. Self-critical thinking ought to encompass the ethics of the story and how the narrative may impact the people and communities being portrayed. Ethnographers need to carefully consider their own backgrounds and the advantages and biases they bring to their work, as these can affect how they understand social situations. While ethnographic accounts should be presented accurately, responsible ethnographers must be aware of how their work can affect others and strive to reduce Ethnographers should continue to collaborate and communicate with the individuals who contributed to the research, to enhance the authenticity of their representations of those individuals' lived realities and voices, ensuring that the research remains responsive, corrective, and cooperative. Ethnographic reflections, like any narrative, should preserve the values of respect, social justice, and compassion in representing people's varied and intricate social realities.

Influence of Personal Narrative

The merging of personal narrative and ethnographic writing is a gradually developing integration. The author's personal story is one that constitutes their lived experiences and feelings, and it is also one that is at risk of being sidelined or submerged. Self-renouncement is, however, founded on questionable grounds, especially when it results in the distortion of the narrative of the people being researched and the narrative of the research itself. The addition of personal stories can make some theories more relatable and easier to understand. By adding their personal stories, an author can help an audience to better understand the individual elements of different sociological frameworks. Furthermore, personal narratives can enable the author to explain their reflexive thought process more easily. This reflexive thought process engages the readers and helps them to understand the author's educational leap. Having said that, the use of personal anecdotes and stories must be balanced and carefully considered in all aspects of the story. Understanding the ethical parameters pertaining to one's biases, objectivities, privilege, and relative social position is necessary for this balance. Furthermore, the ethical principles of potential harm, privacy, and respect for the dignity of participants must be carefully considered. Furthermore, the deliberate use of personal stories must complement and help achieve the ultimate aim of the research. It must not be added simply for the sake of the research. The use of personal stories in the research is more than minor changes in style. It makes it possible for the audience and the author to develop intimate bonds.

The blended use of personal narrative illustrates a complex form of intertwining storytelling. A narrative, when woven carefully, allows a reader to understand not only the sociocultural context of the 'thing' being studied but also the complex internal topology of the researcher. In personal narratives, when constructed thoughtfully and used ethically, there is the power to add to ethnographic writing a level of interest that brings the work alive and fills the chasm that exists, all too often, between academic writing and the 'real' world. The use of personal narrative is particularly profound and serves to 'soften' academic writing, breathe life into a discourse, and, more importantly, create a dialogue or connection with the audience.

Keeping the Audience interested

Keeping the audience interested is a vital part of writing on social life and, as such, deserves careful attention and consideration. The quality of scholarly work is often determined by the extent to which the readers are 'hooked', 'captured' and brought into the web of the social and the human world. This part of the work wants to focus on the different techniques that a writer can use to maintain the reader's interest throughout the story. An essential element of keeping the audience interested is narrative. The use of narratives as vehicles to recount life as it is, together with social phenomena, helps readers gain some profound connection and insight into the heart of the problem. Employing the narrative partly stimulates empathy and critical thinking.

Achieving the proper equilibrium between storytelling and expository writing, masterfully converts academic prose into a thrilling work that touches the audience's hearts and minds. In addition, the appropriate application of imagery and language enhances the text, creating a rich depiction of social life that sparks the audience's interest and imagination. Adding sensory language and other rich words to the text removes the social realities from the pages and prompts the reader to a more personal, insightful encounter with the research. Furthermore, capturing the reader's interest involves the enforcement of a clear and systematic line of reasoning and writing in the delivered document. By combining stories, reasoning, and conclusions, the author can develop a deep continuity that will maintain the audience's attention and even curiosity. Additionally, the shifting of rhythms through quiet, contemplative spaces to vibrant social stories captures the interest of the audience between pages. Constructing a blend of elements and different narratives in the text is an additional and essential tool for improving reader attention. In this way, the author creates a richer understanding of the topic while prompting the reader to step into different human experiences and dialogues that are captured in a narrative.

Knotting these multiple voices together not only furthers the narrative but also broadens the inclusivity and significance of the text for the audience. Finally, the ability to maintain attention is also dependent on the use of rhetorical strategies and a prose style that lightens the text. The use of metaphors, analogies, and rhetorical questioning allows the writer to add thickness and texture to the narrative, compelling the audience to think about it as social. In other words, the authors can use narrative, imagery, coherence, multiple voices, and rhetorical devices to maintain the audience's attention and turn dull academic prose into an exciting journey of exploration and understanding.

***

1. Reflexive Ethnography:

Clifford, James, and George E. Marcus (eds.). Writing Culture: The Poetics and Politics of Ethnography. University of California Press, 1986.

This groundbreaking collection redefined ethnography as a literary and interpretive practice, emphasising reflexivity, authorial positionality, and the constructed nature of ethnographic texts.

Behar, Ruth. The Vulnerable Observer: Anthropology That Breaks Your Heart. Beacon Press, 1996.

The book argues for emotionally engaged, self-aware

ethnography that foregrounds the ethnographer's subjectivity.

Davies, Charlotte A. "Reflexive Ethnography: A Guide to Researching Selves and Others." Routledge, 1999.

The book provides both practical and theoretical guidance on conducting reflexive ethnographic research.

2. Performance Ethnography & Ethnography as Performance:

Denzin, Norman K. Performance Ethnography: Critical Pedagogy and the Politics of Culture. Sage, 2003.

Denzin builds on the work of Goffman and others, arguing that ethnography should be performative, dialogic, and politically engaged.

Goffman, Erving. Frame Analysis: An Essay on the Organization of Experience. Harper & Row, 1974.

While not ethnography per se, this work underpins performance-based understandings of social interaction—key to your reference.

Conquergood, Dwight. "Performance Ethnography: The Politics and Pedagogies of Culture." The Drama Review, vol. 46, no. 2, 2002, pp. 145–156.

Conquergood advocates for embodied, dialogic, and ethical performance-based ethnography that resists objectification.

3. Ethnography as Storytelling and Artistic Composition:

Van Maanen, John. Tales of the Field: On Writing Ethnography. University of Chicago Press, 1988.

This classic text distinguishes between realist, confessional, and impressionist ethnographic writing styles and places a strong emphasis on narrative craft.

Ellis, Carolyn, Tony E. Adams, and Arthur P. Bochner. "Autoethnography: An Overview." Forum: Qualitative Social

Research, vol. 12, no. 1, 2011.

Discusses autoethnography as a form of reflexive, narrative-driven research blending personal experience and cultural analysis.

4. Boundaries, Fluidity, and Interpretive Systems:

Geertz, Clifford. The Interpretation of Cultures. Basic Books, 1973.

The book introduces the concept of "thick description" and approaches culture as a complex system of interpretation that ethnographers must navigate.

Ingold, Tim. The Perception of the Environment: Essays on Livelihood, Dwelling and Skill. Routledge, 2000.

Challenges rigid boundaries between observer/observed and emphasises skilled, embodied engagement with social life.

Law, John. After Method: Mess in Social Science Research. Routledge, 2004.

Discusses "mess" and fluidity in social research, resonating with your phrase, "slosh to systems."

12
Interdisciplinary Resonance
The Interrelation of Various Fields and Disciplines

Interdisciplinary Influence: An Introduction

When exploring the idea behind interdisciplinary influence, it is important to understand the foundational elements behind impact across disciplines. The interrelation of various fields of study transcends the boundaries of academic disciplines and has established some form of mutualism, where knowledge gained from one discipline is interwoven and interlinked with others. Anthropology has and continues to provide useful analogies to disciplines that wish to understand social behaviour and social interactions due to its almost exclusive focus on the study of human societies and cultures. Different disciplines that study social behaviour have been influenced by the ethnographic methodology developed in anthropology, which seeks to observe participants and collect qualitative data to approach their subjects in deeper and more refined ways. This immersion and context-sensitive research has resonated and influenced sociology, psychology, and even linguistics, thereby expanding the methodological scope available to scholars. Moreover, the focus on cultural relativism and the recognition of multiple viewpoints in anthropology has inspired anthropologists to adopt a more inclusive and reflexive approach to interdisciplinary work. The anthropological lessons gained in various disciplines have prompted reflexive researchers to think more in-depth about the context, the relations of power, and the complex relations of meaning that shape social interactions.

These truths remain the same and develop the cross- and

interdisciplinary dialogue for the ever-growing and enriching intellectual co-production world of knowledge.

Anthropology and Ethnographic Strands

Anthropology offers a wide range of integrative elements, including those that support Goffman's dramaturgical theory and provide other aids to enhance behavioural discourse. Ethnographic studies in anthropology correspond closely to Goffman's sociological approach to the study of social phenomena. Using the method of participant observation and cultural immersion, anthropologists study symbolic interaction and societal performances and structures. Ethnographers study different cultures and communities to expose the so-called 'scripts and codes' Goffman refers to in his front- and backstage analysis. In addition, Goffman's description of culture and society as a whole is consistent with the description of his focal point, the society and the 'individual' for the action of his disciplinary branches. All understand that the cultural backdrop is fundamental in shaping the character and behavioural traits of a person within the system of actions. Goffman's violent, constant, continuous and ever-present metaphors deepen our understanding of the social life performance through anthropological study on the ritual and non-ritual acts and symbols.

By investigating these ethnographic terrains imagined by anthropologists, one draws parallels to Goffman's study, which sheds light on the many facets of social engagement.

Further Contributions and Expansions

Within the context of sociology, it is evident that Goffman's influence on the framework of symbolic interactionism is profound. This subsection seeks to analyse Goffman's impact on sociological theory and research, including its extensions, together with the impact that his work continues to have on the discipline. Goffman's study on face-to-face interactions, alongside the dramaturgical analysis and the presentation of self, has been enormously impactful on the sociology of social life. His self as a social constructivist and performer/self as a social context has changed the relationship sociologists have with identity and its construction, including impression management. Additionally, Goffman's perspectives on the influence of institutions on the behaviour of individuals have been useful to sociologists studying organisations, communities, and social structures. Within the context of Goffman's work, sociologists have pioneered and applied it to various social phenomena, including the study of deviance, power relations, and social stratification. In sociology, the concept of impression management has been useful in explaining identity construction with respect to workplace, school, and social media interactions.

The focus of Goffman on the microaspects of social interaction has also stimulated a sociological analysis of social behaviour, social groups, and social relations. In addition, he has had an impact on qualitative research, especially ethnographies and observational work. Goffman has been recognised by sociologists for his attempts to understand social life through close fieldwork, participant observation, and context analysis, thus enhancing social research in many areas of the world. Research using Goffman's work in conjunction with other sociological frameworks has been able to enhance the cross-disciplinary impact of his work and prompted interaction with anthropology, psychology, communication, and even criminology. Such cross-disciplinary interaction has enriched sociological research but has also made it possible to study the interaction of social phenomena in a more complex manner. Goffman's impact on the study of social phenomena has been in suggesting new avenues and approaches to the study of performance and social structures, new sociological research, and new sociological frameworks to work with. Goffman secured ample bases for social research and sociological cross-disciplinary interaction.

Behavioural Sciences and More Psychology

With regard to social interaction, the addition of psychology gives deep structural understandings of the actions of humans and the processes that lead to behaviours. The focus of this section is to weave the behavioural theories and research of psychology with the social phenomena of cognition, affect, and behaviour.

Understanding the role social perception plays in attribution has emerged as one of the primary issues in the analysis of interpersonal relations. Considering how people perceive and assign meaning to the behaviour of others helps to appreciate the complex relationship between psychological phenomena and individual actions and behaviours. In addition, the impact of social norms, attitudes, and beliefs on behaviour reinforces the notion that the psychological and sociological aspects of life are intricately woven throughout. From a behavioural psychology perspective, the complexities of social life are analysed as behaviours. Specifically, we assess the phenomena of reinforcement and social decision-making through the lens of social motivations and responses. Furthermore, the phenomenon of social cognition focusses on the social processes of impression, identity, and role management. Researchers analyse the phenomena of social gestures, which fall under the domain of non-verbal communication, in terms of social fills, as well as gestures, postures, and special expressions that accompany them. Of particular importance, the analysis of behaviours—consequences of social behaviour—offers a perspective of social life that encompasses the sociocultural and psychological dimensions as they are structured and functionally understood in behaviour analysis.

Various psychological perspectives can help understand the impact of emotions, empathy, and social relations, which helps clarify the emotional and affective dimensions of human social life. Carrying out an interdisciplinary approach sheds light on psychological dimensions of social life and grows one's appreciation of the psychological and social aspects of life.

Linguistic Applications in Social Interaction

Linguistic applications influence social interaction and the communication behaviour of people and groups in different contexts in society. Studying language offers profound knowledge about the interactional system of human beings. One of the methods employed in linguistics, discourse analysis, attempts to understand the intricate social relations of language as well as the structures and meanings of it. This part of the study focuses on the interdisciplinary impact of the integration of linguistics and social interaction to demonstrate the interactional impact of the different branches: sociology, anthropology, psychology, and communication. In sociology, language is described as a means of social integration and a stage of domination. Conversation analysis sheds light on the fine details of how people manage social power in their daily interactions.

Additionally, understanding the relationship between language and social identity reveals various forms of language practice, along with their differences and how they reflect cultural identity. This practice, in turn, helps develop essential boundaries for groups and contributes to social stratification. The anthropological view of language use investigates the influence of language in the development of culture, its ceremonies, and the shared ethos. Ethnography employs linguistic dissection of written and spoken texts to distil the deeper symbolic significance of utterances, as well as the non-verbal corollary, to explain the constituents of culture and the underlying social structures. Also, the anthropological studies of linguistic diversity and multilingualism in particular societies provide information on how language within community structures provides contexts for social relations and processes of inclusion and exclusion and negotiation of belonging. In psychology, the use of language has assisted in understanding interrelations of various social processes, cognitions, and emotions. In psycholinguistics, frameworks are developed to explain the processes involved in the production and understanding of language and how people interpret messages, control rhythm in a conversation, and express emotions both verbally and non-verbally. The frameworks developed aid in understanding language disorders, language acquisition, and the influence of language on thinking and perception.

The influence of linguistics on media studies is obvious and informs the construction and communication of meaning in media. Within media studies, framing analysis and semiotic studies utilise linguistic approaches to explain how language manipulates language, audience, and global culture. Studying media linguistics provides an understanding of the power in the representation and knowledge production of mediated phenomena and the dynamics of the knowledge production themselves. The interdisciplinary nature of the application of linguistics to social interaction emphasises the importance of linguistics to the understanding of social interaction, social structure and culture. The application of linguistics by researchers from various fields is a testament to the social nature of language and an invitation to an in-depth study of social and interaction order.

The effect on media studies

Goffman is remembered for several things, one of which is the mediation of media and social interactivities. He undertook a profound analysis of the structure and composition of speech communication, which eventually underpinned his conclusions about the functions and sub-functions of the spoken word and the social functions of speech. As a result, he conceptualised the informational design of social speech communication. Erving Goffman and his works on Instagram performance and its repercussions on mediated self-representation, described by numerous authors, are an emerging framework which is critical for understanding unpublished self-presentations on social media. His conceptual recreation of private and public behaviour helps to understand the raised level of self-filtration and moderated personification of oneself through social media services. Furthermore, the influence of mass media has led him to come up with innovative thinking about meaning in social interactions. Goffman's work on gender and the performances of social stigma is a shed where Goffman has sheltered with women within the stigma that he refers to as the shadow, which every woman with a public life desperately tries to conceal.

By engaging with his concepts, Goffman has allowed media studies scholars to untangle the complex interrelationships between media content and audience behaviours, social interactions, and collectively held worldviews. Further, Goffman's concepts dealing with the digital and the virtual have sketched new paths to research the ever-changing conditions of mediated communication. The understanding of online self-presentation and digital impression management has undoubtedly become one of the key features of the social world today. The Goffman Media Studies cross-interconnections are interdisciplinary in the sense that they not only increase our understanding of mediated interconnections but also stimulate a new cross-cutting media studies approach to the critical analysis of the social consequences of media.

Cultural Studies and Everyday Life

The lens cultural studies offers at the intersection of culture, power, and social life is one of the most powerful critical tools in existence. The impact cultural studies has had on Goffman's work becomes clearer as we transcend the logic of everyday interactions towards the broader sociocultural framework. In this section, we draw on the work of Goffman to examine the impact of cultural studies on his scholarship by focusing on the relevance of everyday life and social reality construction.

Cultural studies encompass much more than mere frameworks of society; people inhabit intricate and multilayered systems of culture, meaning, and power. The focus of social interaction on performance, as emphasised by Goffman, resonates with the dominant concerns of cultural studies. These concern the intricate examinations of experience as people actively resolve the issues of identity, meaning, and belonging in the more structured and routine aspects of their lives.

Cultural studies specifically examines social interaction along with the related practices, symbols, and discourses to highlight the acquired power and skill involved in identity impression management, self-presentation, and negotiation. The alteration of cultural and individual interactions is examined within the context of everyday routines, focussing on the intersection of structural order and subjective experience to define shared frameworks of daily life.

This chapter is inspired by the vast body of cultural studies literature and takes the frameworks of subcultures, counter-cultures, and cultural resistance in their relational context to Goffman's social life dissections. We aim to unravel how individuals perform their identities in relation to culture, as they learn from, respond to, and often challenge various competing cultural codes and their associated norms.

With regard to the impact of Goffman's work and cultural studies, the intersection of power, representation, and inequality, along with the thick relations of culture, identity, and social relations, comes to the fore. By employing a sociological, anthropological, and cultural interdisciplinary approach, we seek to clarify the cultural aspects of social life and the culture of social relations. This study, therefore, illuminates the cultural studies and social life aspects of the self, the other, and the social relations and cultural context of the self. Addressing Goffman's work in cultural studies helps us better appreciate the depth of culture in everyday life, along with the nuances of behaviour and identity that his theory reveals.

Philosophical Underpinnings and Debates

In the case of Goffman's work, the philosophy underpinning it, as well as the controversy that surrounds it, requires a focus on the sociological aspects of his theory and the other sociological aspects of discourse that encompass it. The age-old debate over the nature of being and social order is the focus's core.

Goffman's interactionist perspective remains closely tied to phenomenology and existentialism due to his focus on individual lived experience and the meanings people create in their relationships. Furthermore, the ongoing tension within sociology between agency and structure is evident in Goffman's analyses of social encounters as interactions in which people construct their identities within social restrictions. The interplay between personal agency and societal restraint touches upon classical philosophical questions on free will and determinism and further stresses the interdisciplinary reach of Goffman's work. Moreover, the philosophical aspects of Goffman's dramaturgical approach to social life suggest a need to scrutinise the nature of truth, authenticity, and performance in daily life. Goffman's work has drawn on people's reflection about the social self and self-presentation as a way of contributing to the ongoing debate about identity, impression management, and the existential dilemma of self-disclosure. The ethical aspects of social interactions and the morality of performing social roles also call for philosophical deliberation and suggest issues of virtue ethics, social consequentialism, and rule-based ethics. These philosophical questions not only shed light on the core ideas in Goffman's theoretical arguments but also highlight the continuing impact of his work on the philosophical discourse.

Furthermore, Goffman's ideas crossing into postmodern and deconstructive philosophy underscore the complexity of social realities and meaning fluidity while also addressing multiplicities of meaning and the idea of meaning social reality as open and contingent. The deconstructionist paradigm as an analysis of the social scripts, the social constructs and the various categories and labels, as well as the social action and the social interaction of the act of dominating and the act of being dominated as social visibility and social invisibility, provides insight into social interaction. Everything that has been said and the dialectics of what has been said and what hasn't, presence and authority, absence and subversion, and Goffman's entire analysis of the ontology and epistemology of the ontology of being mean evoking the need for scholars to cross the boundaries of the discipline and provide deep and rigorous accounts and analyses. In all respects and regarding all issues, Goffman's philosophy and the related controversies highlight the contentious ideas he presents. Goffman has succeeded in undertaking a sociological analysis through philosophical means, seamlessly intertwining eclectic philosophies and sociology. Goffman has clearly demonstrated how the interrelation of various traditions, thoughts, and paradigm shifts within sophisticated philosophies highlights his impact on scholarship that transcends disciplines and contributes to the evolution of critical discourse across sociology, philosophy, and other fields.

Methodological Innovations

Methodological innovations have benefited the social sciences through the development of new means to explore and interpret the complexity of human activity and society.

This discussion centres on the evolving research techniques that have shifted the inquiry focus towards social interaction and social institutions. An example of a crucial methodological advance is the use of mixed methods, which combined qualitative and quantitative approaches to social phenomena. Through qualitative methods, including ethnographic research, interviewing, and quantitative techniques such as surveys and other statistical tools, one is likely to have a deeper understanding of complex social phenomena. Moreover, the emergence of digital ethnography and online data collection has transformed the study of online interaction and communities. Large repositories of data permit sophisticated research on social actions and interactions in cyberspace. The merger of computational methods and big data has enabled the study of extensive social patterns and the nexus of globalisation. Advances in neuroimaging methods and psychophysiology have opened new avenues for research on social cognition and social behaviour. These include studying the social, neural, and physiological mechanisms involved in social interaction, which include empathy, interpersonal relationships, and social influence.

These interdisciplinary approaches bring together psychology, sociology, and neuroscience, unlocking new understanding of the mind in its social surroundings. Furthermore, the growing use of innovative visual research methods, like photo-elicitation and video analysis, has expanded the qualitative research arsenal. Visual data enhances conventional text-based methodologies by providing unique perspectives on culture, identity, and social dynamics. Ethnographic film, in particular, has served as one of the most effective ways to document and communicate the complexities of social life, offering a narrative much richer than standard prose. Alongside these developments, new forms of action research and community-based participatory approaches have helped research subjects become active stakeholders in the research process, enabling coproduction of knowledge and fostering social action. Researchers and diverse partners working together in knowledge co-creation can address intricate social problems and defend more ethical and equitable research conduct. Systematic innovation remains a major driver of social research methodology, enabling scholars to examine the rich complexities of the human social world.

Final Thoughts: Merging Disciplines

The crossings of disciplines in the study of social interaction have generated rich insights and offered many avenues for interdisciplinary collaboration.

Upon completing the different courses, it was clear that the Collins might have had a better grasp at life's complexities if they had studied the issues using different disciplines. Adding anthropology, sociology, psychology, linguistics, media, culture, philosophy, and a slathering of other disciplines helped us better appreciate the unique features of social life and behaviour. The central pillar of the resonances of the strike's disciplines is the acknowledgement of diversity in approaches and the richness of the methodologies and theories themselves, some of which are more or less. Employing ethnographies, surveys, different types of interviews, and even some experimental approaches attains an edge in that some social phenomena might be more deeply understood through the crossing of social disciplines. The combination of these approaches in new and dynamic ways makes it possible to tackle a broader range of questions and issues while at the same time deepening the understanding of social life. Further, the interdisciplinary approaches of Colin and his colleagues provided a much-needed fertile ground for the growth of inter- and even cross-discipline fertilisation. The reports of Colin and his colleagues proved that contacts between different disciplines have generated new ideas and insights, and that highly specialised specialists are greatly encouraged to widen their perspectives and actively appreciate the complexities of the social world. Different ways of looking at a subject enable the collapse of the dividing walls between disciplines, resulting in a much clearer understanding about the interdependence of disciplines and the abundant synergy that comes from cooperation between different fields of study.

Bridged disciplines have consequences that go beyond just the academic sector. Placing different angles together allows us to confront the real world's problems with paint and brushes, providing better answers to intricate problems of society. Be it policy, social, or technological spheres, the use of interdisciplinary approaches makes it easier for us to handle the intricacies of present-day issues. To summarise, the interdisciplinary resonance journey drives home the point that inquiry and scholarship with the most integrations are the most valuable. Openness, humility, and readiness to engage with different fields capture the spirit needed for the birth of new intellectual and societal understanding. Journeying around the boundaries of what is known, the bridges that span the discs, which we build, are the valuable tools for new understanding, wisdom, and concern for one another that have been lacking in the world.

***

1. Anthropology's Interdisciplinary Reach & Ethnography as a Methodological Export

Atkinson, Paul, Amanda Coffey, Sara Delamont, John Lofland, and Lyn Lofland (eds.). *Handbook of Ethnography.* Sage, 2001.

A comprehensive overview of how ethnographic methods have been adapted across sociology, education, communication, and health studies.

Hammersley, Martyn, and Paul Atkinson. *Ethnography: Principles in Practice* (4th ed.). Routledge, 2019.

Traces the evolution of ethnography from anthropology into other social sciences, emphasising its adaptability and theoretical grounding.

Agar, Michael. *The Professional Stranger: An Informal Introduction to Ethnography* (2nd ed.). Academic Press, 1996.

Written by an anthropologist working in applied settings, this book shows how ethnographic thinking informs public health, design, and policy—demonstrating real-world interdisciplinary impact.

Emerson, Robert M., Rachel I. Fretz, and Linda L. Shaw. *Writing Ethnographic Fieldnotes* (2nd ed.). University of Chicago Press, 2011.

While rooted in anthropology, this text is widely used in sociology and education, illustrating ethnography's cross-disciplinary methodological influence.

2. **Cultural Relativism, Reflexivity, and Power in Interdisciplinary Contexts**

Geertz, Clifford. *Local Knowledge: Further Essays in Interpretive Anthropology.* Basic Books, 1983.

Geertz's concept of "local knowledge" and thick description has deeply influenced fields like literary studies, law, and psychology by emphasising context and meaning.

Abu-Lughod, Lila. "Writing Against Culture." In *Recapturing Anthropology: Working in the Present,* edited by Richard

G. Fox, pp. 137–162. School of American Research Press, 1991.

Critiques essentialist notions of culture while affirming anthropology's reflexive stance—widely cited in gender studies, postcolonial theory, and sociology.

Bourdieu, Pierre. *Outline of a Theory of Practice.* Cambridge University Press, 1977.

Though a sociologist, Bourdieu's work is deeply anthropological and demonstrates how anthropological concepts (habitus, field, and practice) travel across disciplines.

3. Ethnography in Specific Disciplines

Sociology

Burawoy, Michael. "The Extended Case Method." *Sociological Theory*, vol. 16, no. 1, 1998, pp. 4–33.

Shows how sociologists have adapted ethnographic methods to study institutions, labour, and power—explicitly drawing on anthropological traditions.

Psychology

Cole, Michael. *Cultural Psychology: A Once and Future Discipline.* Harvard University Press, 1996.

Argues for integrating anthropological insights (especially Vygotskian and ethnographic approaches) into psychological theory.

Shweder, Richard A. *Thinking Through Cultures: Expeditions in Cultural Psychology.* Harvard University Press, 1991.

Demonstrates how anthropology reshapes psychology by foregrounding cultural variation in cognition, emotion, and morality.

Linguistics & Communication

Duranti, Alessandro. *Linguistic Anthropology.* Cambridge University Press, 1997.

Shows how linguistic anthropology bridges language studies, discourse analysis, and ethnography—deeply influencing sociolinguistics and communication studies.

Goodwin, Charles. "Professional Vision." *American Anthropologist*, vol. 96, no. 3, 1994, pp. 606–633.

A foundational article in interactional linguistics and workplace studies, using ethnographic microanalysis to study how professionals "see" their worlds.

4. Interdisciplinarity and Knowledge Co-Production

Klein, Julie Thompson. *Interdisciplinarity: History, Theory, and Practice*. Wayne State University Press, 1990.

A seminal theoretical work on how disciplines interact, with case studies showing anthropology's role in shaping area studies, science and technology studies (STS), and environmental humanities.

Barry, Andrew, Georgina Born, and Gisa Weszkalnys. "Logics of Interdisciplinarity." *Economy and Society*, vol. 37, no. 1, 2008, pp. 20–49.

Analyses how interdisciplinary projects negotiate epistemic differences—anthropology often serves as a "mediating" discipline due to its holistic and contextual orientation.

Escobar, Arturo. *Designs for the Pluriverse: Radical Interdependence, Autonomy, and the Making of Worlds*. Duke University Press, 2018.

Draws on anthropology to propose collaborative, decolonial, and interdisciplinary modes of knowledge co-production.

Part IV: Critical Engagements and Contemporary Relevance

13
Critiques and Controversies
Pros and Cons

Goffman's Criticisms

Goffman has widely been considered one of the most important figures in sociology. He has, however, faced his share of criticism. His contributions to the understanding of social interactions are fundamental, yet intense scrutiny from scholars and critics has surrounded Goffman's work. Here, we will explore in detail the theoretical shortcomings Goffman's work has faced, the sociological discourse's significance, and the challenges within the discourse. We will scrutinise the foundation of Goffman's work, assessing the weaknesses and shortcomings of his theories. We will attempt to highlight, and at the same time appreciate, Goffman's contributions to the field of social sciences, especially as he pioneered the frame and dramaturgical analysis. Goffman's work has been the most hotly contested. As a result, this chapter will try to argue the case for a robust understanding of Goffman in terms of balancing both his contributions to the field and his shortcomings. To achieve this, we have dissected Goffman's work and highlighted his shortcomings. This has helped in understanding the depth of sociological theories needed to appreciate the theories within sociology and the understanding to which they can evolve. We approached Goffman's work and the impact Goffman has had on the field of sociology in a manner that has been devoid of any bias. Goffman's work and Goffman's work alone has been understood, and for any reasoning of Goffman's impact, Goffman's work must be criticised, and this is what the sociological boundaries attempt to challenge.

Theoretical Limitations

Theoretical limitations have always been at the centre of concern with Goffman's works, which have been the subject of scrutiny and analysis critical to the sociological imagination. One major criticism seems to be the essence of Goffman's elements of drama theory. Goffman's depiction of self, and the repression and control sociologists have focused on, is said to be lost on the more critical structural and systemic aspects of social and interpersonal engagements. In addition, Goffman's theories that have been accused of the most micro of focuses have been said to overlook the social elements, or the macro counterpart forces, which influence the performance and identity of individuals. Moreover, the pertinent criticism that has sprung from sociologists of the virtual is the limited access Goffman's theories have to interactions with elements and systems of the self and social identities that include multiple and blended local and virtual presentations and a more complex, pluralist, and multiverse model. The theory of stigma, which is central to Goffman's works, has been described as the most sensitive point of Goffman's constructs because it reduces complex explanations of the deprivation of agency of people and communities at the margins of society. The qualitative, which Goffman seems to ignore, is the most critical power, and the impositions that arise from social dominantisms and hierarchies, and the inequalities that they perpetuate – these are the thoughts shared by Goffman's critics. Questions regarding Goffman's fundamental weaknesses have led to grappling with his theory and sparked the emergence of new lines of inquiry that seek to explore areas beyond symbolic interactionism. Thus, considering these weaknesses becomes a starting point for further development of sociology and the deepening of our insight into the intricacies of social life.

Methodological Issues

This chapter addresses the troubling issues with the methodologies of Erving Goffman's works, concentrating on vital problem areas that have been major points for scholarly discourse and criticism. Goffman's methodology is ethnographic and partly participant observation, and it is said to emphasise the difficulties in tapping social interaction. Detractors have been critical about the nature of his observations of the human behavioural tapestry and volume, and they have raised questions about the biases and limitations of his views. Goffman supporters counterchargethe critics by suggesting that Goffman's borderline approach captures the everyday life micro-world interactions; however, with social encounters which acknowledge the fact that structuralism is an argument. A critical area of focus in the discussion is the stance of the researcher within the subject area of inquiry and the social world being studied. Discussions surrounding interactional involvement have been influenced by Goffman's immersionist approach and have triggered consideration about the balance of reflexivity and objectivity in qualitative research. In addition, the ethics of gaze, which pertains to observing and recording social behaviour, has been a focus of critical reflection, raising sophisticated issues related to the ethics of permission, the protection of privacy, observer effects, and the balance of the social situation in which attention is placed. Moreover, a few issues of social behaviour on the interactional level in real life and their record in the form of rendered description have raised some methodological questions. Transcription as a method has suffered a lot of criticism because the presence of lived experience, such as nuances and contextual elements, is often omitted, and thus the narrative is oversimplified. In addition, the question of reliability and validity is often raised in social research about gestures, postures, and embodied behaviour, aiming to reveal the complex social order of the phenomena. In other words, the subject of the research is the method by which social actions are concealed, and the understanding of the method is highlighted. The research aims to focus on understanding cross-border social contact, particularly in relation to Goffman's work.

This part of the research process highlights the challenge of balancing global patterns of social behaviour with culturally specific practices, illustrating the importance of awareness and understanding of context when conducting and interpreting observational research. Resolving these concerns, however, does bring scholars and practitioners into complex conversations, which require continuously refining the methods, drawing from multiple disciplines to address the gaps in the study of social interactions, and balancing rigour and transparency with ethical considerations.

Observed Behaviour Ethics

Observed behaviour ethics are essential in any research aimed at protecting the integrity of subjects and participants, as well as preserving the context of the evidence collected. Within the facets of Goffman's work and the ever-expanding arms of sociology, such ethics take on vital contouring. Ethnographic studies involve complex ethical dilemmas, even in the straightforward process of obtaining informed consent, which may require researchers to minimise their presence in the environment or consider the ethical implications of their presence in related contexts.

Partaking in the elements of the study information sheet and the study consent document is integral to the process. Each pertains to how and in what format the information will be captured and analysed. Each element linked with participation is associated with risks as well as related potential benefits. Along with the study participants, risks also relate to the researchers. Complete respect for the focus and privacy of the subjects must be observed. This means the efforts to not be intrusive as the observations are made and notes taken are crucial. Indiscretions would include oversights, shielding sensitive information from disclosure and unconsented revealing. The PhDs of the researchers and the impact of the observable intrusions of fabric must be taken into account. Knowledge and data in interactions must be in equilibrium with the exposure as well as the impact loss of sensitive and delicate aspects. Thinking beyond the participants of the study for a moment captures the rest of the world, including the cultural and social frameworks associated with the study. All the guiding thoughts and actions to realise the study form the self and become the parameters of the researcher. The subjects themselves become unrepresented subjects of the study with a whole range of unanticipated consequences. As each lies within the ethical dimensions from the principles of the study, a researcher must also define morality within the guidelines. The subjects remain primary stakeholders working with the academic and public domain. The consequences attract ongoing modification, and the rest must lie within the rational actions of the community's feelings. These lie within the possible actions the principles of the study foster. Finally, ethical dimensions are better captured through the principles of reflex and reflection. Each fosters accountability and multi-layer concern of the layers connected, including the very subjective feelings.

Reflecting upon these ethical issues, researchers can achieve respect, beneficence, and justice in their observations "to knowledge and its innovative development", which would be a compassionate development.

Goffman's Gender Analysis – A Critical Take

Goffman's work on gender analysis, like the rest of his work, continues to be received both positively and negatively, and the field of gender theory takes on contemporary clothing. While Goffman's insights on gender performance and identity have influenced the social sciences, his work has also faced criticism for its dominance of intersectionality and its insufficient attention to the diversity of gender experiences.

Critics of Goffman's theorisation on gender, in particular changes of status, claim his work is ahistorical, as it rests on a binary and thus essentialist conceptual framework. There are also others who have pointed to the lack of attention to power structures and functions that govern gender relations and interactions in Goffman's work. By focusing on performance, Goffman is suggesting an almost decontextualised approach to the social, political, and, perhaps, economic relations that pertain to the displaying and receiving of gender. Critical feminists argue that Goffman's work on gender is in need of systematic interrogation to overturn the moral boundaries embraced by it.

They argue that gender identity should be broadened to include more at the margins. Other theorists are or have been in conversations with Goffman's work in an attempt to modernise the gender and sexuality elements. Scholars in gender studies hope to dismantle and reconstruct gendered realities in a more complex way by queering Goffman through queer theory, post-structuralism, and critical race theory. These attempts to fill the gaps within Goffman's treatment of gender involve recognising gender behaviour fluidity, gender performativity, and context. Furthermore, more recent scholarship has underscored the relationship between gender and other dimensions of identity, resisting the tendency to treat gender in analytical isolation. Goffman's work on gender has been reviewed critically to demonstrate the changes that have taken place in gender studies, which urge us to consider more than necessary to be able to understand gender as it works in the world.

Dialogue with Contemporary Theorists

In the process of critically analysing Goffman's foundational works, it is critical to frame them in the context of a discussion with other contemporary theorists. Goffman's works have transcended boundaries and slices of the world while invoking the most fervent controversies among academics regarding social interaction, the performance of identity, and symbolic interactionism. In this chapter, we will address the conversations that occur at the intersection of Goffman's theoretical edifice and the works of other theorists in sociology, anthropology, psychology, and communication. These conversations, on the one hand, testify to the enduring relevance of Goffman's ideas. On the other hand, societal and technological shifts have transformed and changed his ideas. The conversation with other contemporary theorists involves scrutinising the ways in which the intellectual braid of Goffman's works intertwines with those of Judith Butler, Pierre Bourdieu, and other contemporary masters, alongside Michel Foucault and Erich Goffman. The emphasis will be on the interdisciplinary points of contact and divergence with the aim of constructing a hypothesised middle ground where the ideas of Goffman and his contemporaries converge and clash. The purpose is to establish the framework for discussing Goffman's theories in the context of recent social theories in their full complexity.

This examination involves grappling with uses and extensions of Goffman's concepts, which requires assessing contentions and criticisms levelled at his scholarship resulting from theoretical and practical engagement with digital interactivity, mediated communication, and social relations on a global scale. The aim of this examination from the above perspective is to illustrate the ways Goffman's scholarship has prompted, as well as counterposed, social relations in the 21st century. We will also attempt to assess the challenges that lie in the practical facilitation of Goffman's philosophies in light of contemporary issues, especially in relation to the geo-cultural and socio-economic complexities in which they must be situated. Engaging with contemporary scholars provides impetus for a serious reconsideration of the scope of Goffman's theories, broadening the need to reflect on the consequences of oversimplifying theories in relation to such diverse sociocultural realities. This chapter intends to contribute to the understanding of the relationship of Goffman's theories to the advancing domain of social theory, which has yet to be explored.

Global Interpretations and Misinterpretations

When global sociology is concerned, Goffman has been highly influential and controversial simultaneously regarding the reception of his work in different cultures.

As his theories and concepts traversed national boundaries, they faced diverse degrees of acceptance and misinterpretation, leading to a broad spectrum of responses. It is helpful to analyse the interpretations and misinterpretations of Goffman's work globally to appreciate its influence in sociological discussions everywhere. One important point to consider is the different contexts and cultures in which Goffman's work has had an interpretative impact. Some cultures accepted it as a way of theorising cultural social behaviour, while others struggled to find a fit between Goffman's theory and their own sociocultural context. This gap created a set of global interpretations, which range from full support to tempered embrace of Goffman's work. On the other hand, there is also a risk of misinterpretation. Goffman's observations and analyses are very subtle, and it is easy to lift them out of context when discussing other cultures. Such an approach has resulted in some conjectures that misinterpret Goffman's theories and misunderstand his concepts as they are defined in other cultures. Additionally, the impact of globalisation on Goffman's work is also significant. The manner in which sociological thinking has crossed borders has never been witnessed before, and as a consequence, Goffman's work has been subjected to considerable diffusion and assimilation in many countries around the world.

The expansive reach and influence of his ideas have led to a multiplicity of interpretations, enriching sociological discourse and, at the same time, creating difficulties in enforcing accurate representations of them. Global interpretations and misinterpretations of Goffman's works require an approach that is pluralistic and sensitive to sociocultural diversity. It is an inquiry that seeks equilibrium and appreciates the problems of universal application of his theorising, deepening inquiry into the extent to which his ideas travel. I engage with the intersections between Goffman's great works and their reception in diverse parts of the world to gain a greater appreciation for the applicability of his ideas in a world that is changing sociologically.

Controversies in Media Representation

The media's portrayal of Goffman's works is a contentious and intensely debated topic. There is no doubt that the media, in the course of the publicisation of academic works, tend to oversimplify and exaggerate certain ideas, hence losing the essence of the assumptions plastered in the framework. The mass media, in particular, has frequently oversimplified and misinterpreted Goffman's theories, which are the result of rigorous academic research.

The emphasis on media misrepresentation revolves around the risks of neglecting nuance when sensationalising the work of Goffman, particularly in terms of stigma and identity. The extreme oversimplification runs the risk of misrepresenting the populations Goffman studied, reinforcing stereotypes and social stigma. The media's framing and representation of Goffman's work, especially on stigma, has since triggered discussions about the ethical obligations of journalists and producers. There is a fundamental tension between nuance and simplicity that, with Goffman, the public must remain aware of in his work as detailed and not lose the sociological complexity that comes with it. Even the impact of Goffman's work has entered the academy, with scholars monitoring the effects of popularised Goffman narratives on reception and understanding. The media's circulation and restatement of inaccuracies concerning his philosophies have since spurred conversation as to the obligations of Goffman's scholars and institutions to confront and rectify these inaccuracies. This raises the broader issue motivating the discourse on the responsibilities of the academic community itself to ensure that Goffman's theories, and social theory more broadly, are contextualised and systematically engaged with instead of being passively assimilated.

The age of technology has enabled different dimensions of media representation with the exchange of productive dialogue, alongside the engagement of false discourse, on social media and the internet. The public engagement and the academic dimension of the internet, regarding the media ecology, pose particular difficulties in the safeguarding of Goffman's concepts, particularly the ideas and the integrity of Goffman's concepts in the media. The media representation of Goffman's work emphasises its critical importance, which counterbalances the need for proper sociological communication in the ever-growing sociological communication discourse in the media.

Academic Debates and Disputes

Conflict regarding Erving Goffman's work has had an impact on the advancement of the discourse in sociology and symbolic interactionism. Central to these discourses is the argument of how far the theoretical concepts and methods of Goffman can be used in the social world, and how far his ideas claim to warrant recognition and are valid in the context of society as a whole. The central problem of this dispute is the issue of reliability and validity in his works. Goffman is criticised for drawing conclusions which, more often than not, are based on selective, small sets, and his isolative characteristic research does not represent the social world.

Moreover, scholars have engaged in extensive debates concerning Goffman's stance on ethics surrounding certain observational studies, including the impact his research was bound to have on the studied subjects and the presentation of delicate social phenomena with a degree of ethical negligence. Beyond the criticism of his methodology, disputes have revolved around Goffman's use of gender, in which the debates centre on whether or not his gendered lens is sufficient to capture the scope and plurality of gender relations in the modern world. Disputants have called for an increased theoretical understanding of gender to include an intersectional lens, which takes into account race, class, and sexuality. Additionally, the challenges posed by globalisation and the digital age have initiated further debates concerning Goffman's relevance and applicability in a world that is becoming more interconnected. The divide between real social exchanges and digital social exchanges, as well as the impact of the internet on impression management, has become a point of strife within the academy. Recently, scholars from diverse cultural and geographical spaces have added new dimensions to the debates, emphasising the need for contextual reflexivity when employing Goff's work in cross-cultural settings.

The arguments articulated regarding Goffman's work have certainly been a valuable endeavour for scholarly engagement and discourse around the work itself, and have sparked a re-examination of both the weaknesses and the strengths of symbolic interactionism. They remind us that sociology remains a vibrant and unpredictable field. Moreover, sociology still yearns for a fuller, more nuanced picture of social life.

Concluding Thoughts on the Legacy of Controversy

Goffman's sociological imagination inspired such controversy, and for this reason, the legacy of his work will always remain. At this point, looking back, it's important to understand his work not just as a point of theoretical conflict, but as a point of motivation that has incited immense discourse. It needs to be noted that, as much as the social sciences require critical reflections, in Goffman's case, for example, much of the engagement has been around his observations and the ethics surrounding them. Even more, the unresolved arguments concerning gender, as reflected in some of his works, have demonstrated not only the gaps but also the advanced understanding of social interaction that his work has left behind.

The dialogue with these theorists has clarified the development of interactionism and how it relates to other sociological theories. Examining the global discussion and debate of Goffman's work is crucial, as it has shaped scholarship in diverse cultural contexts. The media controversies surrounding Goffman's work were indicative of the difficulties in sociological communications, particularly concerning the tendency to oversimplify these issues and biases in public discussions. Outside of the scholarly scope, Goffman's theories have sparked public debates and discussions; particularly, the criticisms have brought about the lack of social life in the popular, as well as the mass media, used to portray it. Though the rich extent of the scholarly back-and-forth controversies suggests the legacy of controversies is, perhaps, the most important insight to take into sociological investigations, it certainly is also far beyond the branch of sociological works itself. Research and thinking about Goffman's work suggest there is a diversity of perspectives one must tackle, and in doing so there is a dense, complicated sociological framework one is required to embrace. There are sociological controversies that are useful in addressing the criticisms about his major points of contributions and the branch of sociology itself. Critiques serve as a valuable tool for Goffman's deeper engagement as a sociologist.

Encouraging dissent and disagreement helps the discipline advance and grow, and it helps perpetually polish and broaden the theoretical and methodological approaches. Ultimately, the controversy surrounding Goffman's work highlights the strength of sociological thinking, with his legacy being defined by this very controversy. It illustrates the conflict between scathing review and imaginative synthesis, opposition and growth, and the sociological discipline of learning, which is still thirsting today.

***

1. Critiques of Micro-Level Focus and Neglect of Macro-Structures

Goffman is often criticised for focusing almost exclusively on face-to-face interaction while ignoring larger social structures like class, race, gender, and political economy.

Wrong, Dennis H. "The Oversocialized Conception of Man in Modern Sociology." *American Sociological Review*, vol. 26, no. 2, 1961, pp. 183–193.

Though not solely about Goffman, this classic critique targets interactionist theories (including Goffman's) for underestimating agency and structural power.

Collins, Randall. *Interaction Ritual Chains.* Princeton University Press, 2004.

While building on Goffman, Collins acknowledges the limitation of Goffman's micro-focus and attempts to link interaction rituals to macro-social processes.

Burawoy, Michael. "The Politics of Production and the Production of Politics." In *Manufacturing Consent: Changes in the Labour Process Under Monopoly Capitalism,* 1979.

Argues that Goffman's analysis of institutions (e.g., in *Asylums*) lacks attention to political economy and labour relations.

2. Gender, Race, and Power Blind Spots

Feminist and critical race scholars have pointed out that Goffman's work largely ignores systemic inequalities and treats social actors as generic, often male, white, and middle-class subjects.

Smith, Dorothy E. *The Everyday World as Problematic: A Feminist Sociology.* Northeastern University Press, 1987.

Critiques Goffman (and ethnomethodology more broadly) for erasing women's lived experiences and institutional gendered power.

West, Candace, and Don H. Zimmerman. "Doing Gender." *Gender & Society,* vol. 1, no. 2, 1987, pp. 125–151.

While influenced by Goffman's interactionism, they argue his framework doesn't adequately account for how gender is *constituted* through interaction within hierarchical systems.

Alexander, Jeffrey C. "The Strong Program in Cultural Sociology and the 'Performative Turn.'" In *Cultural Sociology,* edited by Lynette Spillman, 2002.

Notes that Goffman's performance model lacks attention to how performances are shaped by cultural codes tied to race, class, and history.

3. Methodological and Epistemological Criticisms

Goffman's style—aphoristic, anecdotal, and often lacking empirical data—has drawn criticism for being impressionistic or unscientific.

Manning, Philip K. *Erving Goffman and Modern Sociology.* Stanford University Press, 1992.

A sympathetic but critical overview that addresses Goffman's resistance to formal theory, his ambiguous methodology, and the difficulty of operationalising his concepts.

Burns, Tom. *Erving Goffman.* Tavistock, 1992.

Discusses Goffman's literary style and tendency toward metaphor over systematic analysis, raising questions about testability and generalisability.

Fine, Gary Alan. "Ten Lies of Ethnography: Moral Dilemmas of Field Research." *Journal of Contemporary Ethnography*, vol. 22, no. 3, 1993, pp. 267–294.

While not solely about Goffman, Fine (a student of Goffman) reflects on the ethical and methodological ambiguities in Goffman's observational approach (e.g., in *Behaviour in Public Places*).

4. Ethical and Political Critiques

Some scholars argue Goffman's work can be politically quietist—describing social order without challenging injustice.

Scull, Andrew. "The Politics of Asylums: Goffman and the Critics." In *Madhouses, Mad-Doctors, and Madmen: The Social History of Psychiatry in the Victorian Era*, edited by Andrew Scull, 1981.

Questions whether Goffman's *Asylums* (1961) led to deinstitutionalisation without adequate alternatives, contributing to the criminalisation of mental illness.

Scheff, Thomas J. *Being Mentally Ill: A Sociological Theory* (3rd ed.). Aldine, 1984.

While influenced by Goffman's *stigma* theory, Scheff offers a more structural and compassionate model, critiquing Goffman for sometimes treating stigma as a game of impression management rather than a source of deep suffering.

5. Defences and Reinterpretations

Several scholars have responded to these critiques by reinterpreting Goffman as more nuanced than often assumed.

Rawls, Anne Warfield. "The Interaction Order Sui Generis: Goffman's Contribution to Social Theory." *Sociological Theory*, vol. 14, no. 3, 1996, pp. 267–286.

Argues that Goffman's focus on the "interaction order" is not anti-structural but reveals a distinct level of social reality that coexists with macro-structures.

Jacobsen, Michael Hviid, and Søren Kristiansen (eds.). *The Contemporary Goffman.* Routledge, 2019.

A recent collection that addresses critiques and shows Goffman's relevance to digital culture, emotions, and inequality—demonstrating his adaptability.

14
Goffman in the Digital Age
Influence and Continuity Beyond His Time

Goffman's Relevance in Modern Times

Erving Goffman is well known for his publication on social interaction as well as self-presentation due to its overwhelming relevance even today. With the technological advancement, such terms and ideas that Goffman developed continue to be relevant in the analysis of today's social phenomena. The growth of technology and the Internet, along with the development of new relational modalities, has changed the landscape of communication and interaction, making it an appropriate moment for applying Goffman's theoretical analysis. In the present day, with cross- and multicultural situations, the Internet allows for the increased complexity of contacts that are made on a daily basis. The expansion of the Internet and social media introduces a new era of communication, allowing for self-presentation and impression management. Through the lens of Goffman's dramaturgy, that is, self-presentation as a performance, we can analyse the processes of identity construction and impression management that occur within the various sites of social interaction. The relevance of Goffman's work allows for a greater understanding of the strategies that people employ in social interactions as well as self-presentation in the complex and dynamic Web of today.

Furthermore, while observing Goffman's work for contemporary significance, it is clear that the newer forms of face-to-face interactions have shifted from the physical world to include a wide range of digital interactions. The combination of spoken and body language and the handling of social etiquette, as well as the manoeuvring of the social graph, digital social graph, and hypertextual spaces, are all relevant elements of current social life. Goffman and the communication studies are all relevant for helping to understand the particularities of communication in the digital world. In addition, the even greater spread of technologies has brought into existence phenomena at the level of society that never existed before, like the loss of boundaries between public and private life, the cultivation of personal pages, and the development of online subcultures. Understanding these kinds of fast-changing sociocultural conditions requires an appropriate theoretical framework. In the case of Goffman, the appropriate frame would be the digital age. Thus, it is Goffman's ideas that stand to gain the most from the introduction of technology, as they not only sustain meaning but also explain the current changes in the complexity of interacting with the rest of the world in a digital format.

Digital Spaces and New Forms of Interaction

Digital technology has changed the interactions and the self-presentation of people in society.

Virtual interaction has developed significantly due to online networks, innovative communication tools, and social media. In addition to allowing people to instantly contact old friends and reinforce existing friendships, social media enables users to form new friendships. Digital communication has removed the physical constraints to social interaction and has transformed the manner in which people express and present themselves. On these various social media platforms, people find themselves in a number of different situations defined by complex virtual social behaviours, each with its own interaction patterns, customs, and signs. In the absence of physical social contact and body language, communication has to be achieved by other means, such as emojis, GIFs, and videos. In addition, the time delay in the response allows individuals to contemplate over the structure to present to the targeted audience; hence, the online persona. The online presence is different from the offline presence and is considered as an avatar by the users. Self-disclosure in the avatar digital space is between the individual and the avatar. The vast hyperconnected digital space allows the sharing of personal experiences and stories with huge audiences, which has resulted in the blurring of personal and social life.

Moreover, the capacity to limit the exposure of some elements of one's life enables the cultivation of an identity crafted with precision, a filtered identity affecting how the online world perceives and engages with the individual. In addition to this, the design of digital systems structures the very form of communication and, by extension, the nature of social communication. Elements such as algorithms, targeted marketing campaigns, and user interactions facilitate the creation of automated systems where users interact with individualised content aligned with their interests and needs. This social framework not only improves user experience, but the formation of these markets fundamentally alters the creation of digital communities with shared beliefs, interests, or affinities. The rapid growth of digitalised environments has also added new forms of social interaction, resulting in increased interconnectedness and visibility. Online social forms, such as social media groups and communities, serve as contexts in which users engage in collective behaviours, rituals, and performances that mimic physical forms. The digital 'subcultures' and 'communities' that emerge serve as containers for complex social systems with unique rules and structures. To sum up, the expansion of online spaces has transformed society by providing new and more profound forms of social interaction.

The relationship between technology and social interaction continues to progress and offers new perspectives for study and scholarly work. From the standpoint of social life and the conclusions of Goffman, understanding the impacts of the digital changes is essential.

The Virtual Presentation of Self

Social media's rise has provided individuals with limitless opportunities to self-curate and share their life stories. From the point of view of self-presentation, social media has changed sociological self-presentation the most. Virtual self-presentation refers to the online identity formation and management that involves the audience and the strategic use of content, images, and language to project a desired online persona. Online, people can showcase the parts of their life that they wish to project and hide or eliminate the unfavourable. This procedure is a clear example of Goffman's theory of social interaction because people tend to manage their self-presentation in such a way that makes them the most positively perceived. People use the technology in various ways for self-presentation, including user profiles, status updates, photo albums, and personal pages.

These platforms allow users to display their skills, accomplishments, and experiences, which usually results in a tailor-made construction of their lives. Thus, virtual self-presentation takes on a performative nature, and the line between genuine and fake becomes blurred. Users have to deal with the contradiction of ideal self and real self that is usable in online interactions. Also, there is the added difficulty of the online world in the control of one's virtual self-presentation. Situated at the convergence of the real world and the online world is the matter of control over one's identity and the online realm, which raises issues over privacy, consent, and the consequences of data permanence. The social boundaries and interactions are transformed by the ability of cyber interactions to move beyond physical interactions, which calls for change in the social boundaries and existing etiquettes. Also, the ability to communicate instantaneously and asynchronously requires a greater understanding of the consequences of one's actions that pertain to social media online within cyberspace for one's permanence. With regard to the self-virtual presentation, Goffman's theories help to understand the digital interaction in a certain performative context. The concepts of front stage and backstage, to some extent, lose their original context as people have to deal with the public and the private parts of their self online. Also, facework is apparent in the behaviour undertaken to deal with positive reputation preservation in the case of possible reputation-damaging activities.

As we equip ourselves with Goffman's understanding of human interactions and self-construction within the developed and developing digital structures, we need to reflect on the self phenomena beyond the individual canvas within the boundary of the virtual self. This is especially true with the issues of capturing the reality of virtual life and the trust associated with them and the secondary layers of social stratification they elicit within the digital domains. Issues of online self-presentation are, indeed, self-enclosing, but the consequences of self-exposure online are broader. Online stigma is the cloak of Goffman's presentation of self in the age of virtualisation. The social stigma that arises on account of social differences, deviance, and non-conformity, and attribution to secondary labels, such as being an immigrant, an artist, or a minority, is a variation of online stigma.

Online Stigma and Social Identity

When social distance is increased and anonymity is present, cyberspace stigma becomes a novel phenomenon that self-identifies as a complex of self and social constructions. The state of being stigmatised in the virtual world and concealed within domains of a non-identifying avatar in cyberspace identifies patterns that paradoxically unite layers of structural reality and self-structured perceptions. The digital age also parleys opportunities to stilt fantasies of diverse avatars.

Despite this, they enjoy the freedom of anonymity while still facing the risk of unchecked bias and unwarranted discrimination. In the quest to maintain an online image, people attempt to avoid stigmatisation by identity work that governs the sense of self by meshing with the social norms and values of a given society. In addition, social media has resulted in increased efforts to meet fictitious standards of beauty, success and lifestyle, which, in turn, has resulted in greater self-surveillance and a more active pursuit of social approval. Such self-sponsored images do not only affect the self but also serve to shape society's self-understanding and social order of an object while reinforcing stigma and the social exclusion of people in the context of the internet. From a social interactionist perspective, the digital social world provides a venue in which people do seem to exercise stigma through derogatory remarks, social exclusion, and weak forms of aggression. In addition, the ability of people to stigmatise others while being unexposed physically and emotionally, the likelihood that the stigma would, at some point in time, circulate over vast social networks, and the tremendous risks of social, digital and permanent reputation damage demonstrate that the world is interconnected and people's behaviour impacts others. Understanding the forms of online stigma and how they shape social identity is a vital concern in today's digital world.

Through the synthesis of virtual surroundings with socially structured frameworks, policymakers and scholars alike may find methods to embrace, address, and cultivate online discrimination and foster compassion. Furthermore, applying social identity theory, the stigma bearers' experiences of being online 'marked' can help understand resilience, coping, and the fostering of ruggedness in relation to the digital challenges.

Total Institutions in the Cyberspace

In his work, 'Total Institutions', Goffman describes how people's lives in particular social settings are organised and controlled in the most elaborate ways. In the digital era, total institutions are online communities, social networks, and virtual systems where people exist and are absorbed into thick, all-encompassing layers of rules and regulations. In the online world, there are some digital environments that have the attributes of total institutions and can dominate the pattern of people's behaviour, social transactions, and self-construal. Goffman's foundational articulation of total institutions places emphasis on unqualified nuances, behaviours, protocols, and governance that hierarchise the net. Such platforms as online discussion groups, virtual realities, and multiplayer online games are total participant spaces where, dominantly, the flow is controlled and interactivity is allowed in some aspects.

Appropriately, the power dynamics and prescriptions of visibility and control in 'normal' total institutions are mirrored in the monitoring, surveillance, and algorithmic governance of the digital sphere. In these total cybernetic institutions, the geographical divisions of public and private space dissolve; individuals inhabit a zone of differentiated scrutiny and assessment, where their behaviour and speech are monitored and judged around the clock. The employees of these digital institutions are in a situation of continuous monitoring, the social and technical apparatus of which deeply transforms their feeling of self-rule, privacy, and freedom in the digital space.

Social dynamics in the blockchain environments of total institutions also provide access to the construction of alternative subcultures, identities, and symbolic universes, which is also observable in the sociological patterns of physical institution settings. In these cases, people learn how to socialise and create their own systems of norms and power in the digital world, just like Goffman's shielding social units, which brings us to the same observations reported by Goffman.

Focusing on and analysing the total institutions of cyberspace is imperative for integrating the digital sociological imagination with the new social realities. The intersection of technology and social engagement calls for a study of how these virtual total institutions have changed people's behaviours, identities, and daily life activities.

Recognising digital total institutions helps shine a light on the intersections of technology, culture, and society while helping us gain a better understanding of the complex ways in which people live today.

Rituals and Norms in Digital Communication

As with any new form of communication, such as digital communication, new practices and norms regarding our behaviour in the online realm are established. In this instance, individuals participating in a digital conversation may cross certain boundaries through silence, which conveys meaning and reflects the norms of digital communication. As digital conversations have participants, those involved will orient themselves both at the beginning, by greeting, in the middle, by expressing thanks, and at the end, by saying farewell.

Norms also concern attitudes, moments, and the messages themselves in sociocultural communications and new platforms. Emoticons, emojis, memes, and GIFs are some forms of digital symbols. These express silent communication visually, transcending theology and symbols of unspoken discourse. In addition to rituals, digital communication has also given rise to actions and interactions within online social communities. These include netiquette and the new behaviour termed 'trolling', with digital communication social norms being certainly more complex than those of other forms of communication. People think they are in space.

The adoption of social norms shapes the construction of online personas and the reputation associated with them. A digital identity is normally tailored to the norm of self-expression, while self-promotion is encouraged in every social environment. The digital reciprocity norm is another striking example of digital social behaviour. Users acknowledge each other and respond to social engagements with reciprocal likes, shares, comments, and follows. This reciprocity not only shifts attention and the range of content, but it is also vital for community building and the sense of cohesion in online social networks. The development of influencers and other digital personalities of interest illustrates the reflexes of social engagement and attention on the web. New social systems defined by sociologists as "influence networks" form a new social order based on the interplay of social activity on the web. The development of such behavioural systems in digital communication reveals the elaborate rituals and mechanisms underlying social life on the web.

Studying sociology helps us better understand digital societies, as it enables scholars to discern the patterns that shape behaviours, interactions, and experiences within the boundless cyberspace.

Frame Analysis in the Context of New Media

Applying Erving Goffman's sociology Frame Analysis concept, we shall attempt to explain its application in the context of the digital phenomena actuated by new media.

Goffman's sociology, particularly in frame analysis, explores the engagement possibilities with new media. Within the digital environment, people engage and transcend multiple levels of frames in ways that vary the experiences and interactions they undertake. Much like the theatrical frames that Goffman describes, the elements within a digital context or screen create a virtual environment where social interactions can occur. In this environment, people frame, create, and assign meaning to what exists on the screen or computer.

It is worth noting, however, that computing possesses its own distinct range of complexities and opportunities as individuals engage in the defining processes of impression management, which includes intricate elements such as the maintenance of boundaries and the construction of perceived realities within the multi-layered digital environment.

The implications of Goffman's focus on the performative aspect of interactions are one of the reasons why scholars are trying to extend frame analysis to new media. In addition, the presence of new media in society necessitates an investigation into how frames are constructed and disseminated on different media. Individual and social processes of framing are exemplified in social media and discussion groups as well as in different types of cyber communities, whereby the framing is enabled, shaped and constrained by the social, cultural, and technological context. The availability of electronic communication to all is perhaps what makes the study of how social, cultural and technological frames are constructed, maintained, challenged and renegotiated in this context so invaluable. Moreover, one of the areas in which people are strategic in the use of frame adaptation is described by Goffman's concept of keying. The way Goffman describes keying is, for me, an illustration of the different (dominant and recessive) frames that determine and are realised in the online behaviour of individuals. People blend different types of keying to negotiate self in social interaction in a way that fits the dominant frames in the online world.

The use of keying within new media analysis offers new territory for research in performance, digital identity, and the intricacies of framing, as well as multiple, concurrent, and complex negotiations. Overall, Goffman's frame analysis provides sophisticated tools for untangling the new media puzzle. As they examine the interdigital frames, personal agents, and the rest of the world, scholars analysing Goffman's work are preserving the evolution of thinking about the complex structures of digital culture and including the virtual self in relation to the ever more complex disengagement of self in situated online interactions.

Exploring Gender Dynamics Online

While engaging with the complex activities of the online world, it becomes obvious that the issue of gender is crucial.

The internet is an intriguing space with a relative abundance of data and information on the methods and techniques of performance, construction, and negotiation of gender identity. Social media and even online games are a rich source of gendered activities. This part of the work explores gendered relations in the internet space, analysing the subtle and complicated aspects of an area that is still developing. One of the critical components of research on gender relations today is the self-presentation of the individuals in the digital spaces.

The performative aspect of gender appears as users shape their digital selves by avatars, profiles, status updates, and other interactions. This self-presentation often mirrors external reality based on sociocultural frameworks and gender stereotypes. Looking at the language, images, and stories in self-presentations can reveal much about the nature of gender construction in the virtual world. At the same time, gender plays a significant role in digital communication and power relations. Documents have shown the existence of different treatments, such as cyberbullying, online harassment, and other forms of discrimination that are gendered. These scholars have had the opportunity to examine the extent to which gendered behaviours shape the quality and experience of online interactions. Also, there is the need to address how gender amalgamates with other components of identity, such as race, sexuality, and class. In addition, the development of new online communities has led to new forms of gender socialisation and belonging. Whether in virtual support groups, forums, or networks based on shared interests, participants engage in gendered behaviours that both conform to and counteract social norms. These communities' dynamics of inclusion, exclusion, and solidarity provide a rich ground for research and theory.

The Gender Dynamics in the Digital Age Study, like any other, must start with the technological infrastructures themselves. Exclusionary practices and gaps in the gender spectra must be analysed, particularly focussing on algorithmic biases in recommendation engines and other digitally discriminatory interfaces that are designed with flawed mental models. Understanding and addressing the uneven technology-mediated gendered opportunities and experiences will help in advancing more equitable and inclusive digital environments.

The research spanning gender relations in digital environments, and more broadly the geography of inquiry technology, sociology and psychology, encompasses a lot of branches. Thus, to tackle the core of the problem, a deeper understanding of the relations between gender and technology needs to be established, as well as the social issues that arise from the matter, to provide a solution to this gap.

Methodological Innovations in Observing Digital Interactions

New challenges and demands arise as the number of digital interactions increases. Hence, it has become increasingly urgent to develop new methods to analyse and comprehend interactions that are taking place online. Social research on these interactions should not be confined or limited but rather should evolve to analyse the essence of even the most sophisticated online behaviours. To develop a more comprehensive framework for the analysis of digital interactions, one must combine and synthesise traditional qualitative and quantitative research with newer methodologies appropriate to the virtual world.

A significant aspect of observing digital conduct is the use of analytical and visual data tools. These tools help researchers identify correlation patterns, trends, and associations from the complex data sets produced by digital engagements. Using these big data sets, researchers can understand the functioning of digital communities, sociograms, and individual behaviours. Moreover, the use of highly specialised computational tools, such as natural language processing and sentiment classification, provides a better appreciation of the digital engagements and the emotive elements accompanying such interactions. Another important aspect of methodological innovation is the application of ethnographic techniques to the digital space. Traditional ethnography involves deep immersion and field participant observation, while its application to the digital world requires the practitioner to probe and socially navigate the web, interact with various online communities, and identify the boundaries of the digital culture that dictates such engagements. These changes require a new form of ethical reasoning regarding what informed consent means and the part the researcher is allowed to play in the observation. Moreover, digital reflexivity in research that involves social interactions requires at a minimum disciplinary versatility, which in this case means a profound understanding of digital interactions.

Anonymity, along with the fluidity of digital platforms, is both a benefit and a challenge at the same time. The challenge is building trust, forming relationships, and verifying the truthfulness of digital personas. It brings to the fore and raises the questions of digital dualism. The intersection of the online and offline personas, which overlap and diverge in complex manners. The intersection is not the focus of this particular piece, but the digital dualism that spans across both the online and offline personas hinges largely on the visual and multimedia facets of interaction. The understanding of digital interaction is largely visualised, and the analysis of various forms of multimedia user-generated content, including but not limited to photographs, videos, and even memes, provides a deep contextual analysis of the visual and content rhetoric that underpins and informs the meaning of the various digital messages. There is a need to develop pioneering and innovative strategies to describe and explain the layers of meaning arising from the visual content in question, which are also essential for understanding the visual vocabularies used in online conversations. The content discussed above encapsulates the essence of innovative methodologies for understanding digital interaction, which involve capturing and processing multi-layered data, and thus remain flexible by integrating both the latest frameworks and traditional ones. The complex nature of digital interaction is greatly simplified from the sociocultural phenomena that define the shifts and changes attributed to the evolving scope of research being done in the social sciences.

Conclusion: Bridging Traditional Insights with the Digital Era

Evaluating the social implications of Goffman's work in the modern world, it is clear that the ideas and arguments that form the basis of Goffman's work are far from obsolete. In fact, they are even more useful.

The adjustments to existing methods of observing interactions on digital platforms provided new understandings regarding the intricacies of social interaction, as their relevance intersects quite elegantly with some long-standing traditions. Goffman's ideas of self, as well as the analysis of social roles and rituals, seem to have integrated quite well with the digital world. The virtual self on social media, discussion forums, and in virtual reality illustrates Goffman's theories on impression management and identity performance. Furthermore, the online stigma and social identity indicators found in online communities behave the same way as in the face-to-face world, which shows how Goffman's methodology still resonates in the digital world. Furthermore, the total institution concept has a physical manifestation but also includes digital spaces, such as in the case of gaming, social platforms, and virtual communities, which people tend to occupy. These digital spaces, together with their structural components, as well as the flanking behavioural norms and rituals, provide an easier way to understand Goffman's studies of institutional life.

Originally intended for face-to-face conversations, frame analysis has been adapted for online communication, shedding additional light on the construction and negotiation of meaning online. Goffman's remarks about the performance of gender roles offer an enhanced understanding of the complexities of gender dynamics in the online world. The advanced methods designed for the observation of digital interactions have allowed researchers to apply Goffman's principles of social behaviour to the internet and sharpen their understanding of online social behaviour. The continued relevance of Goffman's theories to the 21st century is a testament to their relevance for understanding the complex social relationships of modern life. Scholars and applied specialists are in a position to develop new avenues for interdisciplinary social research by bringing together core theoretical concepts and modern digital social challenges. This is a timely opportunity to integrate Goffman's perspectives with the new trends in social behaviour in the increasingly interlinked digital age.

***

1. Digital Spaces & New Forms of Interaction
Boyd, Danah. *It's Complicated: The Social Lives of Networked Teens.* Yale University Press, 2014.
Uses Goffmanian ideas to analyse how teens navigate identity, privacy, and audience in social media.
Marwick, Alice E., and danah boyd. "I Tweet Honestly, I Tweet Passionately: Twitter Users, Context Collapse, and the Imagined Audience." *New Media & Society*, vol. 13, no. 1, 2011, pp. 114–133.
Introduces "context collapse"—a digital-era challenge to Goffman's front/back stage distinction.
Papacharissi, Zizi. *Affective Publics: Sentiment, Technology, and Politics.* Oxford University Press, 2014.
Reimagines publics through affect and performance, extending Goffman's dramaturgy to networked communication.

2. The Virtual Presentation of Self
Zhao, Shanyang, Sherri Grasmuck, and Jason Martin.

"Identity Construction on Facebook: Digital Empowerment in Anchored Relationships." *Computers in Human Behaviour*, vol. 24, no. 5, 2008, pp. 1816–1836.

Applies Goffman's *Presentation of Self in Everyday Life* to profile curation on Facebook.

Davis, Jenny L., and Nathan Jurgenson. "Context Collapse and the Public/Private Divide." In *The SAGE Handbook of Social Media*, edited by Jean Burgess, Alice Marwick, and Thomas Poell, 2018, pp. 317–332.

Updates Goffman's front/back stage for algorithmic platforms where audiences merge.

Ellison, Nicole B., Charles Steinfield, and Cliff Lampe. "The Benefits of Facebook 'Friends': Social Capital and College Students' Use of Online Social Network Sites." *Journal of Computer-Mediated Communication*, vol. 12, no. 4, 2007, pp. 1143–1168.

Shows how users strategically manage impressions to build social capital.

3. Online Stigma and Social Identity

Goffman, Erving. *Stigma: Notes on the Management of Spoilt Identity* (1963).

Foundational text—essential for any analysis of digital stigma.

Duguay, Stefanie. "Lesbian, Gay, Bisexual, Trans, and Queer Visibility Through Selfies: Comparing Platform Mediations of Self-Presentation on Instagram and Vine." *Social Media + Society*, vol. 2, no. 2, 2016.

Examines how LGBTQ+ users navigate stigma and visibility using Goffman's framework.

Tiidenberg, Katrin, and Emily van der Nagel. "Selfies, Image and the Re-Making of the Body." *Body & Society*, vol. 23, no. 3, 2017, pp. 77–100.

Analyses how marginalised bodies negotiate stigma and agency in visual self-presentation.

Lup, Zizi Papacharissi, and Maria de Fatima Oliveira. "Affective News and Networked Publics: The Rhythms of News Storytelling on #Egypt." *Journal of Communication*, vol. 62, no. 2, 2012.

Discusses how stigmatised groups reclaim narratives in digital spaces.

4. Total Institutions in Cyberspace

Andrejevic, Mark. *iSpy: Surveillance and Power in the Interactive Era.* University Press of Kansas, 2007.

Argues that digital platforms function as "soft" total institutions through data extraction and behavioural control.

Zuboff, Shoshana. *The Age of Surveillance Capitalism.* PublicAffairs, 2019.

While not explicitly Goffmanian, her concept of "instrumentarian power" resonates with critiques of digital total institutions.

Brayne, Sarah. "Surveillance and System Avoidance: Criminal Justice Contact and Social Marginalisation." *American Sociological Review*, vol. 79, no. 3, 2014, pp. 367–390.

Shows how digital surveillance (e.g., social media monitoring) extends carceral logics into everyday life—akin to Goffman's institutional control.

5. Rituals and Norms in Digital Communication

Sumner, Emily R., et al. "#SorryNotSorry: The Art of the Non-Apology on Twitter." *New Media & Society*, vol. 20, no. 12, 2018, pp. 4689–4707.

Analyses face-work and ritual repair in online discourse.

Tolmie, Peter, et al. "'It's Just a Social Network!': The Interactional Organization of Social Media Use." *Proceedings of the ACM on Human-Computer Interaction*, vol. 1, no. CSCW, 2017,

Article 54.

Uses ethnomethodology and Goffman to study how norms emerge in platform use.

Gibbs, Martin, et al. "The Social Affordances of Social Media for Grieving and Memorialising." *New Media & Society*, vol. 17, no. 2, 2015, pp. 253–269.

Explores digital mourning as ritualised interaction.

6. Frame Analysis in the Context of New Media

Goffman, Erving. *Frame Analysis: An Essay on the Organization of Experience* (1974).

Essential primary source.

Bucher, Taina. "The Algorithmic Imaginary: Exploring the Ordinary Affects of Facebook Algorithms." *Information, Communication & Society*, vol. 20, no. 1, 2017, pp. 30–44.

Updates frame analysis for algorithmically mediated realities.

Gillespie, Tarleton. "The Relevance of Algorithms." In *Media Technologies: Essays on Communication, Materiality, and Society*, edited by Tarleton Gillespie, Pablo J. Boczkowski, and Kirsten A. Foot, MIT Press, 2014, pp. 167–194.

Shows how platforms shape frames of interpretation—extending Goffman's key insight.

7. Gender Dynamics Online

Marwick, Alice E. *Status Update: Celebrity, Publicity, and Branding in the Social Media Age.* Yale University Press, 2013.

Uses Goffman to analyse self-branding, with attention to gendered performance.

Mendes, Kaitlynn, Jessica Ringrose, and Jessalynn Keller. *Digital Feminist Activism: Girls and Women Fight Back Against Rape Culture.* Oxford University Press, 2019.

Examines how feminist activists manage stigma, visibility, and audience online.

Duffy, Brooke Erin, and Emily Hund. "Gendered Visibility: Examining Influencer Marketing and the Discursive Construction of the 'Ideal' Female Influencer." *Social Media + Society*, vol. 5, no. 3, 2019.

Analyses gendered impression management in influencer culture.

8. Methodological Innovations in Observing Digital Interactions

Pink, Sarah, et al. *Digital Ethnography: Principles and Practice*. Sage, 2016.

Offers updated ethnographic methods for studying digital life, including virtual participant observation.

Hine, Christine. *Ethnography for the Internet: Embedded, Embodied and Everyday*. Bloomsbury, 2015.

Proposes "connective ethnography" to study fluid online-offline interactions—directly engaging with Goffman's legacy.

Markham, Annette N., and Elizabeth Buchanan. "Ethical Decision-Making in Online Social Research." In *The SAGE Handbook of Online Research Methods*, 2nd ed., edited by Nigel Fielding, Raymond M. Lee, and Grant Blank, Sage, 2017, pp. 278–294.

Addresses ethical and methodological challenges in observing digital "front stages".

Beneito-Montagut, Roser. "Ethnography Goes Online: Towards a User-Centred Methodology to Research Online Social Interaction." *Qualitative Research*, vol. 11, no. 6, 2011, pp. 715–732.

Develops Goffman-inspired methods for digital fieldwork.

9. Theoretical Syntheses

Jacobsen, Michael Hviid. "Goffman in Cyberspace: Interaction, Ritual, and Self in the Digital Age." In *The Contempo-*

rary Goffman, edited by Michael Hviid Jacobsen and Søren Kristiansen, Routledge, 2019, pp. 253-274.

Directly addresses your core question—how Goffman's framework holds up online.

Couldry, Nick. "Theorising Media as Practice." *Social Semiotics,* vol. 14, no. 2, 2004, pp. 115-132.

Bridges Goffman, Bourdieu, and media practice theory for digital contexts.

15
Legacy and Future Directions
Enduring Relevance

Understanding Goffman's Lasting Influence

The works of Goffman are crucial to the development of sociology and have profoundly influenced many other fields of study. He managed to illuminate the complexities of social interactions in various ways and changed the direction of sociological thinking. His spell on the theoretical development of the subject is unquestionable. With works such as 'The Presentation of Self in Everyday Life' and 'Interaction Ritual', he offered new ways to understand the depth of human behaviour in society.

In sociology, his self-presentation, impression management, and dramaturgical analysis have made the first steps in grasping the detailed structure of sociological performances. His further development of the concept of social stigma and identity has shaped the discourse on deviance and social psychology. His influence extends beyond sociology, encompassing anthropology, psychology, communication, and even organisational studies. All these disciplines have used his works to understand the complexities of interpersonal relationships and the subtle mechanisms that lie within social structures.

Goffman's works are still relevant, and they provoke new discussions, re-evaluations, and critiques. Even after decades, they still seem to sustain their power and invite discourse.

Influences on Sociological Theory

Slowly and surely, Goffman revolutionised how sociological theory would be shaped and taught. It became apparent how his approach changed the understanding of social interactions, identity, and the realities formed on a daily basis. Sociologists became able to study behaviour with the help of Goffman's impression formation, self-presentation, and dramaturgical framework. More than the reality social interactions portray, Goffman made it easier to study the underlying processes. Each of the complex interactions taking place led to these social phenomena. Goffman is a gifted thinker, and he clearly illustrated these findings with his concept of the "interaction order". Fundamental to his theory, Goffman insists face-to-face meetings and interactions are crucial. Goffman's theories are built on the principles of hard studies, and he explained social system behaviour with sophisticated frameworks. By defining and dissecting social structures and their interconnections, Goffman helps define and comprehend social order and the social relations at play. Equally, Goffman's study on stigma and identity has left a mark on sociological theorising. Discourse on identity transformation and the management of self, pertaining to how socially isolated and stigmatised individuals put their identity within the social system, has generated immense scholarship and has led to further study on social exclusion and marginality. Goffman's examination of total institutions, like prisons and mental asylums, has also added to our appreciation of the social system and its workings as well as the behaviour and self-image of the subject.

Goffman has had an impact on sociology. His influence reaches inter- and multidisciplinary sociology, social psychology, and communication, as well as cultural studies. He has helped to understand the articulation of society and the individual, micro and macro interactions, by providing a theoretical explanation of the relation of social structures and individual interactions. His work has also showcased the relation of social structures to the individual. His work places the individual at the centre and enhances the understanding of the sociology of individual action. His work has also contributed to enhancing performativity studies as well as the social life of the individual.

The impact of Erving Goffman on sociological theory is profound and works on many different levels.

As a responsive and responsible scholar, Goffman constructed and expanded theoretical frameworks while simultaneously situating those frameworks rigorously in real-world events and changes. His works have inspired a myriad of researchers to look closely and explore sociological elements in everyday life down to their most intricate details. Goffman's scholarship has almost universally been the foundation on which new research gets constructed and is, therefore, a permanent fixture in the world of sociological thought and empirical investigations.

Influence in Anthropology

Within the field of anthropology, the works of Erving Goffman have inspired a rethinking of how much culture and society are seen to operate. His new ideas on the self have greatly helped in the understanding of culture and social identity construction and social etiquette running within the boundaries of various cultures and ethnographic settings. Goffman's theories on performative behaviours, facework, impression management, and symbolic interactionism have aided in the better understanding of social behaviours and their interrelations in diverse cultures and contexts. His works have also shown the importance of studying emotional behaviours, which have encouraged students and scholars of anthropology to study the rituals of social relationships and the underlying structures of social order.

The works of Goffman have motivated anthropologists to take extra care when it comes to studying social traditions, kinship, and relics, thus assisting in better grasping the intricacies of different cultures. In addition, Goffman's study of culture's performative dimensions has influenced anthropologists to examine rituals, ceremonies, and everyday activities in their performative and symbolic aspects. This has improved understanding of the symbolic and functional communicative aspects of culture, increasing awareness of the elaborate apparatus through which people articulate, assert, and contest identity in different social contexts. The works of Goffman still motivate anthropologists to study the micro-sociology of social interactions and the new interrelations that come from the close interrelation of social existence. As more anthropologists try to come to terms with the problem of culture in the context of globalisation, Goffman's works have always provided the motivation and the intellectual sensitivity required in grappling with important issues in human culture and social interaction.

Goffman's Contributions to Psychology

The frameworks that encompass Goffman's theories pertaining to self-presentation, self-impression management, and the micro-sociological facets of social interaction have been key insights into the psychology of individuals and human behavioural patterns. Many psychologists foundationally base their works on 'facework', 'dramaturgical theory', and other concepts that Goffman developed. Goffman has skilfully articulated the social world as a complex relational system that individuals manoeuvre for the construction of multiple social and personal identities and public/private self-roles. Moreover, Goffman's treatment of everyday life as having a performative quality has helped advance the psychology of nonverbal communication, particularly the social signs of posture, gesture, facial expression, and other social attention to self-movements. Lastly, his study of symbolic interaction and meaning has helped unravel the constructive processes people employ to develop a common world and decode social reality. Goffman has profoundly shaped the appreciation of social cognition, social and identity construction, and relational systems by providing rich empirical contexts and theoretical frameworks for advancing research and theory. Goffman's writings have also instigated psychologists to reconsider the more basic assumptions they hold concerning human agency and social impact by questioning social roles, relations of power, and the social order in connection to the individual.

His interdisciplinary approach has allowed for comprehensive discussions spanning sociology, anthropology, and psychology, which promoted the integration of diverse theories and practices. For contemporary psychologists who wrestle with identity, social interaction, and the individual and group's self, Goffman's legacy has enduring significance for fresh inspiration and intellectual challenge. There are abundant avenues for studying behaviour and the intricacies of human behaviour and psyche.

Applications in Modern Communication Studies

Goffman's influence on modern communication studies is of utmost importance and adds an invaluable frame of reference for studying different facets of human interaction. Goffman's impact is not only about traditional physical interaction, but in the present digitally interwoven world, his ideas are equally relevant in the complex realm of online communication and social media. It is in this context that self-presentation and impression management in online communication are critically important. Goffman's front-stage and backstage behaviour apply well to social media and virtual avatars and profiles, where self-presentation is optimised. His insights on the construction of identity narratives and community performance in networks and online virtual worlds are equally important.

One more important area is the study of non-verbal communication and self-communication. Goffman's focus on body language, gestures, and facial expressions serves the study of how social meaning is generated and how social relations are constructed in communication at a distance. Further, Goffman's idea of framing and the management of interactional 'frames' can be used to study how communication is organised in various digital modalities. The idea of 'frame' in particular is useful in capturing the logic of meaning and understanding construction and sharing in asynchronous online communication. Also, Goffman examines the impact of technology on communication social norms, etiquette, and the formation of online communities. Applying Goffman's approach to modern studies of communication, we illuminate the growing body of literature that attempts to account for the complexity of digital interactions and the processes of identity construction and performance in relation to online environments.

Contributions to organisational behaviour

Goffman is widely regarded as one of the most prominent sociologists of his time. His intellectual prowess remained unmatched within the sociological community. His insights into sociological ideas were grounded in the phenomenological school of thought, which provided the lens through which he designed his primary sociological concepts. Such primary concepts included social interaction as performance and the social theatre. It was these ideas that provided the initial introductions to understanding the complexities of how people involved in a professional sphere engage with the dynamics at play, as well as how social roles are performed and constructed. Goffman himself provided sociological insight into the phenomena of the self. His self-concepts, considered part of the self-sociological frameworks, suggest that individuals believe their attempts to establish themselves in social interactions transcend typical social norms. This collision in social is where the concept of an individual having social masks to cover different elements of their being comes to life.

Goffman's analytic lens focused on how working individuals in a professional environment relate to one another and how they manage these social interactions as primary phenomena. He established foundational processes for understanding the work environment. Such processes include the elements of showing performance, which are facets of social engagement covered under non-verbal interaction, and the outcomes that sprout from these interactions, also called the social economy as a whole. Additionally, Goffman is understood and widely appreciated for his teachings on non-verbal dynamics and interaction engagement. He also put forth invaluable understanding of the types of engagements that prevail among people in a workplace. It is here that he posits that people in the working environment grapple with the dual struggle of interaction and performance, which leads to the phenomenon that is equilibrium among order, chaos and anxiety.

Goffman provided a sociological theory that examines the social performances occurring within the workplace, highlighting how they are influenced by the social economy. The performances are within what Goffman classified as the levers of the masks, and the social economy is the automation that drives these levers. The social economy pushes individuals to perform. It is in such moments when the automatic systems in place within the economy of social interactions prompt individuals to think, act, and perform that equilibrium duplicates order and chaos, and social performance takes place in a burst of anxiety.

The distinction between external roles and internal functions provides additional insights into the challenges of modifying and protecting one's self in light of the impositions set by the organisation. Furthermore, the attempt by Goffman to analyse 'team performance' and the relations of individual contributions to the group's work has increased the understanding of and the organisation of work relations within the organisation. His ideas about self-presentation in a workgroup and the relationships of solidarity in a workgroup have contributed to the development of ideas about leadership and team building in the contemporary situation. Goffman has also focused on the symbolic nature of ceremonies and rituals in the settings of work, which is a continuation of concern with organisational behaviour that has, in turn, focused attention on the performative elements of organisational life. His research on the rituals of meetings, presentations and the celebration of work has helped to expose the ritualistic nature of organisational life, which has shaped ideas about the social structure of work settings and the symbolism of organisational processes. The work of Goffman on organisational behaviour enables contemporary scholars and practitioners to appreciate the complex social relations, impression management procedures, and the underlying organisational culture in the functioning of contemporary work settings.

Enduring Relevance in Cultural Studies

As we explore the lasting significance of Goffman's work in cultural studies, it is evident that his remarkable insights continue to provide frameworks for understanding the nuances of actions across diverse cultures.

Multidisciplinary as it might be, cultural studies has much to gain from Goffman's notions of identity and impression management, social front and social backstage, and the social construction of self. His ideas on culture, identity, and society cross-sections make it much easier to comprehend how people assume and adapt to different roles in varying cultural contexts. Of Goffman's concepts, the analysis of interpersonal contact in different forms of subcultures and looser communities has surely been one of the most impactful. His ideas on stigma and the social interaction theory of the presence of difference have cast some light on power and cultural context inequality in the absence of some issues that many prefer to avoid. Additionally, Goffman has done much to advance cultural studies through the emphasis on everyday life as performance. This has triggered much-needed attention to culture's rituals, ceremonies, and other forms of cultural expression that may have been heretofore considered peripheral. Goffman's ideas on frames, for instance, have offered new ways to think about the shape and the cultural order of meaning and interpretation. Using such an approach, cultural analysts can examine how interaction as well as social and cultural production through different ways of framing and reframing can construct, perpetuate, and contest a culture's politics, ideology, and belief systems.

This approach encourages richer engagement with the intricacies of culture and how people accept, oppose, and reconstruct different cultural phenomena. Critical reflexivity is one of the most important aspects of Goffman's legacy in cultural studies. It encourages self-awareness in the agency/society expectation balance. Studying the self across cultures allows scholars to analyse the roles and impacts of cultural scripts, narratives, and symbolism in constructing and reconstructing personal and group identities. Applying Goffman's approach pushes scholars to think critically about the shifting boundaries of culture, meaning-making in multicultural contexts, and the role of the digital and global world in culture-bridged communications. Goffman's cultural studies legacy is rooted in the profound understanding he gave about performative cultural practices, the dynamics of identity in different cultures, and the relationship between personal will and the structure of culture. His work is still relevant because he captures the nuances of performative cultural practices, the layers of interaction, and the meaning of culture in the digital age.

Critiques and reevaluations

When examining the work of Erving Goffman, it is important to review the various critiques and reevaluations offered in the field of sociology and its neighbouring disciplines.

Critics have expressed concern regarding aspects of Goffman's work. These include the possibility of Goffman having personal bias in his observations, the relative usefulness of some theoretical models, and the applicability of his conclusions in various cultural contexts. Then, concern has also been expressed regarding the depiction of the subjects of total institutions and the ethics of research involving the studied subjects of such institutions. It is such critiques that have induced a rethink of Goffman's work in the scholarly world. There has been intense discourse regarding the critiques and the way Goffman's work is understood to try to form the intricacies of his work. There has also been a growing concern with the need to research the applicability of his ideas to the current world with the development of technology, shifts in social attitudes and a changing world culture. These reinterpretations are indicative of a desire to add to the body of knowledge regarding interactions and behaviours. Furthermore, the growth of interdisciplinary studies has led scholars to look at Goffman's work in the context of other fields, like psychology, communication, and even anthropology. This cross-disciplinary work has shed more light and enabled the re-evaluation of Goffman's work in relation to other areas of scholarship.

The critique and re-evaluation of Goffman's work sheds light on new and creative attempts at the investigation of social phenomena. As new technologies and digital platforms emerge, more researchers, both in Goffman's work and elsewhere, are beginning to reconceptualise how data is collected, analysed, and interpreted. This shift in progress is key to resolving Goffman's older critiques and updating the ideas and concepts he has on the modern world. This scholarly focus on constructive critique and self-reevaluation illustrates the fact that Goffman's work is still much in use today. His arguments have been shown to extend beyond their original boundaries, which gives rise to ongoing discussions regarding the attempts to guide the next phase of sociology.

Innovative Methodologies for Future Research

In an attempt to refine Goffman's legacy, innovative methodologies for future research offer new ways to consider social interaction and behaviour. As Goffman's work continues to evolve, emerging methodologies offer fresh opportunities to deepen our understanding of the dynamics of human interaction. One such methodology is the use of advanced technologies in virtual reality and digital ethnography, which allow the construction of controlled social interaction scenarios and any social virtual environment for the observation and analysis of social behaviour. These tools enable the researcher to collect and analyse the real-time interactions and behaviours of people in virtual environments and other imagined settings. Researchers can study this data in relation to real-world social phenomena.

New methods also arise from within the analysis of big data sets. The advancement of the digital age has created the need to capture massive data sets of interactions and the correspondence of enormous swathes of users across different platforms. Computer methods, such as natural language processing, network analysis, and even linguistics, enable the capture and analysis of previously unseen behavioural complexities. This form of analysis permits researchers to understand micro- and macro-relationships of the phenomena. Participatory and interdisciplinary research are among the most promising methodological frontiers for the study of the social. By blending cognitive, social, and behavioural sciences, scholars face new challenges in enriching social phenomena and understanding the behaviour behind them. The augmentation of social science students will help to broaden perspectives and introduce new imaginative approaches. For example, social print and neural scan frameworks will provide useful insights into the social brain and assist with the psychological phenomenon of the behaviour gap. Furthermore, social and community-driven research frameworks provide new avenues for integrating diverse perspectives into the study of social phenomena. Researchers believe that collaborating with everyday life participants leads to a more equitable and comprehensive understanding of the social phenomena under study.

By engaging in discussions with multiple parties, researchers are able to create new knowledge and produce ideas that relate to the realities of various groups in society, resulting in a richer understanding of the complexities of social interactions. This new creative and innovative research approach is critically important for advancing Goffman's work and for the further development of sociology.

Not only do these new approaches enhance the methods available for studying social interaction, but they also enable researchers to tackle difficult, contemporary problems with greater nuance and sophistication.

Potential Directions for Future Scholarship

Continuously expanding the discipline of sociology and advancing the research on Goffman brings with it new possibilities. Of particular interest is Goffman's work on social phenomena and the currently developed world, focusing on the use of digital technology and the performance of identity, as well as social interaction rituals. With the rise of social networking sites and virtual social environments, there is ample opportunity to explore the ways in which people manage the presentation of self and engage in attitude management in cyberspace. Additionally, there is a need for research on the intersection of Goffman's work with new and emerging technologies such as virtual and augmented reality and the impact of these technologies on social interaction and the construction of social identity.

Researchers need to expand Goffman's theory by applying it to different cultures and marginalised communities. Drawing on intersectionality and critical race theory, they might examine stigma, identity work, and social order in new socio-cultural contexts. This work would enhance our comprehension of social power, oppression, and resistance, guiding initiatives to mitigate social inequality and foster inclusion. Furthermore, Goffman's principles continue to be relevant in new domains, such as therapeutic interactions and healthcare. Close studies of social interactions in clinical settings could elucidate patient-provider relationships, communication, and identity construction processes, informing the design of patient-orientated care improvements. There also remains work to be done on Goffman's theory in the area of organisational behaviour, focusing on remote work and online collaboration. Such investigations might illuminate the presentation of self in work, teamwork, and leadership in digital contexts, providing insights for managers, employees' mental health, and organisational culture.

To conclude, future research should focus on the integration of Goffman's work with cognitive science, linguistics, and human-computer interaction. Collaborations across disciplines would enhance our understanding of social behaviour, social thinking, and social technology to achieve richer and more sophisticated studies of the interaction order in today's world.

***

I. Foundational Assessments of Goffman's Legacy

Manning, Philip K. *Erving Goffman and Modern Sociology.* Stanford University Press, 1992.

A classic interpretive overview that situates Goffman within 20th-century social theory and traces his influence on symbolic interactionism, ethnomethodology, and microsociology.

Burns, Tom. *Erving Goffman.* Routledge, 1992.

Part of the "Key Sociologists" series; offers a concise yet deep analysis of Goffman's core ideas and his ambiguous relationship with formal theory.

Fine, Gary Alan, and Philip Manning. "Erving Goffman." In *The Blackwell Companion to Major Social Theorists*, edited by George Ritzer, Blackwell, 2003, pp. 490–519.

Summarises Goffman's contributions and lasting impact across disciplines.

Rawls, Anne Warfield. "The Interaction Order Sui Generis: Goffman's Contribution to Social Theory." *Sociological Theory*, vol. 14, no. 3, 1996, pp. 267–286.

Argues that Goffman's concept of the "interaction order" constitutes a distinct and irreducible level of social reality—central to his legacy.

II. Goffman's Influence Across Disciplines

Drew, Paul, and Anthony Wootton (eds.). *Erving Goffman: Exploring the Interaction Order.* Polity Press, 1988.

A seminal collection by leading sociolinguists and conversation analysts showing how Goffman shaped discourse studies and ethnomethodology.

Goffman, Erving. *Interaction Ritual: Essays on Face-to-Face Behaviour* (1967).

Though a primary text, its influence on Randall Collins' *Interaction Ritual Chains* (2004) demonstrates cross-generational theoretical development.

Alexander, Jeffrey C. *The Drama of Social Life: A Dramaturgical Approach to Sociology.* Routledge, 2019.

Extends Goffman's dramaturgy into cultural sociology, showing how performance underpins collective identity and social change.

III. Contemporary Reinterpretations & Future Directions

Jacobsen, Michael Hviid, and Søren Kristiansen (eds.). *The Contemporary Goffman.* Routledge, 2019.

Essential reading. This volume brings together leading scholars to explore Goffman's relevance to:

Digital culture and social media

Emotions and affect

Gender, race, and inequality

Surveillance and control

Methodological innovation — Explicitly addresses "where Goffman goes next".

Tillmann-Healy, Laurel M. "Goffman in the Internet Age: Revisiting the Interaction Order." *Symbolic Interaction*, vol. 43, no. 3, 2020, pp. 357–375.

Examines how digital interaction challenges and extends

Goffman's model of co-present interaction.

Couldry, Nick. "Theorising Media as Practice." *Social Semiotics*, vol. 14, no. 2, 2004, pp. 115–132.

Integrates Goffman with practice theory to analyse media rituals in the digital era—pointing toward future syntheses.

IV. Goffman and Emerging Challenges: Inequality, Ethics, and Technology

Marwick, Alice E., and danah boyd. "Understanding Privacy in the Age of Context Collapse." In *Privacy in Context*, edited by Beate Roessler and Dorota Mokrosinska, Cambridge University Press, 2023.

Builds on Goffman to analyse how digital platforms disrupt traditional front/back stage boundaries—highlighting new ethical and social dilemmas.

Andrejevic, Mark. "The Hidden Camera: Goffman, Surveillance, and the Politics of Visibility." *Surveillance & Society*, vol. 19, no. 1, 2021, pp. 1–14.

Reinterprets Goffman in light of mass data collection, arguing that digital surveillance turns everyone into both performer and watcher.

Wacquant, Loïc. "Goffman's Place in Social Theory." In *Body & Soul: Notebooks of an Apprentice Boxer*, Oxford University Press, 2004, pp. 225–238.

Reflects on Goffman's relevance for embodied sociology and the study of marginality—suggesting pathways for integrating micro and macro analysis.

V. Critical Reflections on Limitations and Evolving Relevance

Smith, Dorothy E. *Institutional Ethnography: A Sociology for People.* AltaMira Press, 2005.

While critical of Goffman's apolitical micro-focus, Smith acknowledges his insights into everyday interaction—urging a more politically engaged extension of his work.

Burawoy, Michael. "Revisiting Goffman's Asylums in the Age of Neoliberalism." *Critical Historical Studies*, vol. 7, no. 2, 2020, pp. 273–297.

Re-examines *asylums* in light of contemporary carceral and digital institutions, showing how Goffman's institutional critique remains urgent.

16
Last Reflections
The Enduring Power of the Interaction Order

Interaction Order

The introduction order of the interaction framework advanced by sociologist Erving Goffman posits great historical and theoretical importance sociologically. This situates them between microsociology and symbolic interactionism. Goffman's interaction order framework offers a critical approach to understanding the nuance and complexities surrounding human interaction within close physical proximity. Understanding the essence of these concepts and their core tenets requires recognising the importance of the historical context that led to them. Goffman traced the interaction order to human social behaviour and the social making of everyday life in a range of institutions. This analysis highlighted the intricate system of implicit norms, rules, gestures, and performances that characterise these social interactions and constitute the interaction order. The interaction order theory remains rooted in the engravings of Goffman's insights about symbolic interactionism and dramaturgical thinking. Self-presentation and impression management remain integral parts of the constituent elements of social encounters.

Moreover, the interaction order is based on the idea that social reality is created through shared meaning and interpretation, as people work together to maintain the meaning of their daily interactions. Goffman's careful study of the details of social behaviour, as well as the social relations themselves, represents the foundation for the interaction order. By assessing the historical context for the interaction order, as well as the origins of its theory, one appreciates the order's capacity to explain social life and its enduring influence on sociological thought.

Fundamental Concepts and Theoretical Foundations

The analysis of the essential aspects and theories is essential to Goffman's Window Theory. Accordingly, the essential aspects and theories of interaction are social order actions that sustain and perpetuate sociological structures. These aspects relate to the social undercurrents of human behaviour within the context of social relations. This part aims to explain the interaction order by synthesising and integrating multiple domains, including sociology, psychology, anthropology, and communications. This section covers the main interactionist and constructionist theories and the mind's social theatre.

These paradigms are fundamental to understanding the principles that guide people's behaviour in different social contexts. In this regard, the section explains the interrelationship between people and the social systems in which they function. In particular, it explains how these systems intertwine to produce the complexities of social behaviour. In addition, the section analyses the intersection of different theories, illustrating their interrelated role in constructing the interaction order. It examines the major literature of scholars and theorists in the field not just to sketch the theoretical contour but also to give the readers a clear understanding of the theoretical approaches to the interrelated phenomena of human interaction. Moreover, the section undertakes exhaustive studies of primary constituents such as self-presentation, impression management, facework, and role theory. These are the foundational elements of Goffman's framework, and they are instrumental in understanding social acts and the meanings they carry as symbols.

This chapter explains the importance of these fundamental ideas in explaining the complexity of human behaviour and in disentangling the 'interaction order' as a complex construct. In this regard, this chapter offers a scholarly excursion to the theoretical foundations of how Goffman describes the interaction order, explaining the fundamental theoretical components that set the boundaries of social interaction interplay and offering the readers a profound level of understanding.

Dynamics of Social Interactions

The foundation of human ties and the workings of society rests on social interaction. To unravel the intricacies of social life, phenomena that social scientists, particularly sociologists, deal with, understanding the social phenomena of the order of interactions becomes critical. At the very intersection of social interaction lie the fundamental elements of complex forms of communication, understanding and reaction. The interaction order includes verbal and non-verbal communication, movement and action, and emotional and facial behavioural responses and reactions, which result in a social activity constructed in forms of inter-behaviour. In sociology, the interaction order emerges as a world phenomenon that attempts to capture the social circumstances of behaviour. One important element is reciprocity. In social relations, there is a continuous cycle of a give-and-take process, where the responses that a counterpart exhibits towards the actions of the interactional partner are exchanged.

Whether it is a conversation, shared activity, or cooperative undertaking, the give and take of the reciprocal and reciprocating exchanges of a conversation is an intricate and complex tapestry of the society's social embroidery. Moreover, the transactions of power and the power structures behind social relations are critical to the manner in which the individual self is performed in different social environments. It is a well-known fact that power differentials will determine the manner in which the actors in a conversation will speak, the decisions to be made, and the social order to be followed. The context of each particular situation will include social structures and order, which are vertical. The context of particular societies and communities will determine different orders of social structures wherein mores, rules, and styles of communication will determine the exchanges of social transactions. These culturally dictated social orders of behaviour guide their members in the use and appreciation of the gestures and social ranks sanctioned in specific cultures. Social interactions and relations are also situational and impacted by the emotional level. Social exchanges need emotional sensitivity and a perception of emotionally appropriate behaviour. These reactions are social because they transcend the immediate situation and weave social threads together. With social exchanges that are resonating emotionally and empathetically, the transcending social threads need to be deeply woven to create tighter and finer connective structures. To understand the social relation phenomena and its structure and contents, the influence of the context and environment is crucial.

Social interactions can occur in various geographies, such as in person, in public or private, on the job, or online. Each has unique traits characterised by the imposed or self-imposed restrictions on the relationships, while the former may range from informal smoothness in random meetings to stiff etiquette in organised meetings. In the end, one has to know the parameters of all these different sociological interactions to decipher the complex relationships a person has. The more complex these elements of argument are, the more potential insight is offered into the structures of argument. In the sociological framework, social interactions are on the more complex end of the spectrum. These interactions, as well as the web of socially interlaced behaviours, self-restraint and observances which define the social order, are the focus of the paper.

Order in Everyday Practices

Order in Everyday Practices is a chapter that focuses on Goffman's emphasis on sociological arguments constructed within routines. The duplicity of elements is central to grasping social order, self-restraining structures, and socially intertwined behaviours. One can detail and construct the gross order of inanimate and unsocialised elements in and around everyday life, element by element. Behind the orderly chaos of a supermarket, self-evident rituals are performed, often unnoticed by the everyday practitioner. These are all the principles that can be maintained, detailed, and restudied so that the foundation of social behaviour can be hidden from the everyday practitioner.

Goffman's scholarship prompts us to contemplate how people cope with these moments of order with grace and flexibility through the use of all sorts of impression management techniques, often to "get by" in society while simultaneously retaining their identity. The concept of "face" becomes prominent as people work stealthily to stay within positive social perception as they navigate the complexities of daily life. Goffman's work reveals to us how the daily routine activities that most people take for granted are meticulously crafted and imbued with social significance and, in all delicate manners, dictate our actions and responses. He attempts to unravel the 'interaction order' to offer insight into the rituals and unspoken behaviours of social life that bind us and provide stability. In attempting to integrate the microsocial acts that constitute our daily lives, Goffman asks us to consider how these interactions enrich social life, shedding light on the intricacies of social behaviour and structure. Goffman's 'Order in Everyday Activities' should be mastered, along with all other elements of society, to help simplify order in our complex world.

Rituals and Their Significance

Rituals comprise a collection of actions, marks of importance, and behaviours of great significance. These define the social interactions and provide a perception of order to different cultures and societies. These beliefs and customs are central to a culture and are very beneficial to a society over a lengthy period. It could be an old-fashioned ritual or a commonplace set of actions. These actions are integrated with ritual feelings. Actions could be basic but endowed with significance.

These actions, ceremonial or monotonous, serve an important meaning within a community because of the positive emotional or psychological affinity they foster for the whole group. They provide a psychological sense of control, the organisation of life, and comfort even in the face of malign certainty.

The recitation of wedding vows and the practices followed in mourning are examples of rituals that help participants structure and work through feelings and reactions to life's events while providing comfort in togetherness and ritualised practice. The meaning of rituals is not limited to participants alone; it communicates ancestry and a part of cultural identity. Societies defend their cultures with their unscripted and scripted rituals and pass the ritualised aspects of civilisation down to later generations. Rituals serve as an anchor to civilisation and a multifaceted prism that provides a scope of reflection on the sets of attributes that form a particular social community. While rituals serve the purpose of social cohesion, it is important to note that the same rituals may also serve to exclude and diminish the value of those ritual conductors that are considered 'different'. The practice of a set of rituals may rather unjustly establish social relations of dominance and subordination within the practice of exclusion, making it embraceable and varied. It is important to recognise the tension between inclusion and exclusion created by the uncompromising impact of rituals within a community, as this tension contributes to forming a diverse social structure. In conclusion, rituals serve as the foundation of social interaction and, consequently, the structure of interactions, influencing societal order, relationship networks, and cultural continuity.

Framed in this manner, the data underscores the relevance of information and cognitive processes, weaving in personal sub-narratives and overarching constructs.

Nonverbal Communication and the Unspoken

The role of nonverbal communication is vital to the social world, often expressing ideas that words cannot. People express feelings, thoughts, and emotions through various forms of non-verbal communication, such as facial expressions and body posture. These unspoken expressions are paramount to the building of social bonds, the exercising of compassion, and the meaning-making of relationships. In addition, they assist in managing social interactions and subtly alter the balance of social power and control. These core social functions are important for understanding social order. In social interaction, communication is predominantly nonverbal. In such instances, communication is nonverbal, messages are exchanged, and meanings are derived and claimed. The subdivisions of communication studied under social dynamics, such as social proxemics, social kinesics, and social paralinguistics, illustrate these concepts. Proxemics, for example, studies the distance in communication and its social and cultural ramifications within interactions and relationships. Kinesics encompasses the collection of disciplines that help explain how body movement, gesture, and facial action communicate and interact with words in various distinct and aligned systems of meaning.

Paralinguistics entails studying the voice in terms of its elements (tone, pitch, and speed) and the emotions it harbours and expresses. In addition, nonverbal communication includes the behaviour of the individual but also the intrinsic meaning of material things and situational context. Artefacts arrange spaces; the manipulation of physical spaces and the formation of behavioural environments carry hidden meaning constructs that shape the social behaviour and interaction of the social sets within that space. These social sets determine who will interact and engage in social actions and how. These sets are interconnected, and their interpretation and recognition are crucial to understanding the interaction order. Furthermore, the integration of verbal and nonverbal communication emphasises a more general form of social interconnectedness. Usually, non-verbal communication accompanies, contradicts, or reinforces verbal communication, regardless of the context in which the speech is uttered. A person skilled in nonverbal communication is regarded as one who possesses communication competence, as well as an understanding and insightful attitude in varying social contexts. Thus, an analysis of nonverbal communication and the unexpressed parts of interaction enriches the study of social behaviour and social relations and clarifies the persistent and extensive presence of nonverbal elements in the interaction order.

Balance of Power and Agency

The balance of power and agency is a constant in the social relations that intertwine and interlace.

Dominating and organisational systems manifest and employ power's relational aspects, which structure and streamline interactions throughout society, institutions, and private relationships. These forms of power are interrupted and contradicted by the autonomous action of agency, which is the ability of an individual to act without hindrances. This chapter addresses the nuanced aspects of the relationship between agency and power, clarifying how these two components complement and conflict with each other within society. Power consists of manifest and latent forms of control that regulate social order and individual conduct. Social control exercises, whether from an organisational position, money, or social expectations, dictate how people behave with one another. Power dynamics are present in every interaction, from subtle cues and gestures to the more comprehensive, complex choices of decision-making. How power functions within social relations, in terms of disempowerment or oppression and, on the other hand, empowerment or advocacy, is important. Agency, in opposition to power, represents control that a person is able to wield over their environment or the individual's ability to make decisions. Social structures are much easier to transform through negotiations and resistance with power.

As individuals attempt to navigate the boundaries of their lived realities, the balance of power and agency elucidates the relational disparities, the level of self-advocacy, and the lived experiences they attempt to forge. Additionally, agency enables individuals to deconstruct oppressive systems, initiate transformations, and establish more equitable social structures. In this case, the primary objective is to explore real-life examples to demonstrate the power and agency intertwined in social systems. Focusing on organisational power dynamics to understand how oppressed social groups exercise their agency in the face of systemic wrongs, the inquiry will illustrate the intersection of these enduring components of society. It will also examine the ethical implications of the use of power and the ethical obligations that accompany the exercise of agency, aiming to demonstrate the need to promote responsible and ethical behaviour across a range of social relationships.

This section attempts to shed the appropriated understanding of the relational balance of power and agency. The study of these phenomena in sociology is more advanced and offers a more critical examination of the consequences on social interactions, arguably and reflexively. In this regard, this study intends to draw primary implications about the need to promote equity, justice, and mutual respect in the context of complex and intricate relationships among human beings.

Interpersonal Relationships Across Contexts

With the assistance of Goffman's frameworks, contextually defined interactions, merged, construed, and meticulously tailored, can be understood and greatly expanded upon within Goffman's paradigms that explore the roles of an individual in a social, multifaceted matrix of relationships. Such frameworks enable consideration of the multitude of differences within an interaction and the gradual, steady emergence of change within distinct syntheses of hitherto established, maintained, and understood societal matrices. Such attending social and personal facets can blend within a novel, unique global context. Definite social spaces and casual environments exhibit complex matrices of interactions, each of which contains a unique social fabric. Such distinct social fabrics persist at defined social and personal levels. Such distinct social and personal levels of behaviour and interaction may be addressed directly within the context of technology as a social and personal behaviour influencer. Goffman's understanding and foresight elucidate the imprinting nature of technology on social and personal behaviour, coupled with interaction norms that used to be rigid and unwavering across relationships and interactions. It is technology's determination and weave across the defined social norms within theories of interpersonal relationships that remain remarkable in the context of Goffman's observations and commentary.`

Drawing from Goffman's scholarly architectural bases, it tries to disentangle the web of personal action and situational limitations that form the web of human social relations. Additionally, the role of interpersonal dependence is examined in various contexts, including nonverbal communication and symbolic acts. This part attempts to provide a detailed account of the changing form of social relationships. It also reinforces the importance of Goffman's work for understanding social relations and the profound impact of social context on interpersonal relations.

Challenges to Interaction Order in Modern Society

The advancement of modern civilisation has significantly altered the nature of social interactions. A popular one arises from interaction. Digital communication has changed the ways people communicate. The shift from nonverbal and verbal communications to online communication has greatly diminished interpersonal communications. Additionally, digital communication, influenced by advanced technology, presents numerous distractions that hinder meaningful contact.

This array of distractions competes for focus, which, in turn, could lessen the quality of social interactions, leading to superficial relationships. The unequal social order in modern society's interactions is profoundly challenged by socio-economic differences. The widening income gaps, coupled with differences in the resources within people's reach, could hinder the development of social relationships anchored in harmony, which bears negative ramifications on the social cohesion of communities as well as societal integration. The almost ubiquitous social media, with its reinstatement of certain norms and values, has added a layer of complexity to the interaction order. The need to fit in, to undoubtedly curated versions of themselves for social media, tends to encourage a certain level of inauthenticity within social interactions. As a result, this creates a space filled with shallow interactions, lack of connection and outright disconnection. Additionally, contemporary society's extremely fast pace tends to foster stress as well as the feeling of time scarcity, which, in turn, interferes with the quality and sufficiency of relationships. People have become so busy that they lack the time and energy to foster interactions that matter, and this weakens social order. The globalised society of today has multiple cultures with varied norms and practices within one society, which leads to social interactions filled with confusion and discord, as well as a lack of developed common social understandings.

The issue of interacting with cultural diversity requires more advanced levels of intercultural competence, which is an important obstacle to seamless and coherent methods of interaction. To address these interconnected issues, we need to reconstruct and rethink the foundation of the interaction order in our modern world. This procedure includes applying new approaches aimed at preserving the authenticity and richness of interpersonal relationships and protecting the enduring influence of the interaction order in our current world.

Conclusion: The Lasting Influence of Goffman

Erving Goffman is one of the first authors to write about the interaction order, and his primary focuses in the area of sociology are in his works about the deep impact he has on how people relate to one another and how people relate to the world around them. By closely examining social life, Goffman unravelled the intricate social structures that shape our daily interactions and highlighted the subtle aspects of social life that we often overlook. Goffman's sociological imagination is at the centre of his enduring influence. The patterns and structures he describes intertwine micro-social everyday life and social institutions.

His sophisticated disaggregation of the performative dimension of social engagement has provided fresh approaches to understanding the symbolic workings of different social environments. No one else has demonstrated the importance of grasping the performative aspects of social behaviour, as Goffman has. He strove to capture the dynamics of sociation and self that were prevalent in his time and the consequences his ideas hold for the present day. Even now his observations about the construction of identities, as well as their management, and the multiple social roles people perform in the world, are of striking importance. Conversely, Goffman's observations have become even more relevant due to the constant advancement of technology and the proliferation of new communication methods and digital interfaces, which change and transform communication and social interaction. The Paradox of Technology Goffman developed himself as an astute sociologist by offering groundbreaking insights about the relation between social interaction and non-verbal behaviour, as well as mediated contact and computer-generated social environments. The integration of the two worlds is a fertile area of inquiry that allows the construction of theories about the interaction of the real and the virtual. In that context and in considering the world that is offered to the people today, Goffman invites us to reconsider the implications of his work for today's world. The interaction order, the flow of interactions, and the dynamics of change and stability within a relational system remain central questions in Goffman's work.

The enduring significance of his work lies in its capacity to serve as a guiding light for theorists, students, practitioners, and even laypersons navigating the perpetual intricacies of social existence. To sum up, the long-lasting influence of Goffman is a reminder of the enduring impact of his original work on sociology. He encapsulated the temporal and spatial dimensions of the interaction order, which is a crucial aspect of sociological understanding. He did this in a way that remains a foundational piece for sociological scholarship.

***

Goffman, Erving. "The Interaction Order." *American Sociological Review*, vol. 48, no. 1, 1983, pp. 1–17.

This is Goffman's definitive statement on the interaction order as a distinct, foundational domain of social life—autonomous from institutions, personalities, or macro-structures. He argues that face-to-face interaction follows its own rules, rituals, and moral obligations.

Key Interpretations & Defences of the Interaction Order

Rawls, Anne Warfield. "The Interaction Order Sui Generis: Goffman's Contribution to Social Theory." *Sociological Theory*, vol. 14, no. 3, 1996, pp. 267–286.

A landmark article that defends Goffman against critics who claim he ignores structure. Rawls argues the interaction order is a *sui generis* (unique) level of social reality that *enables* all other social forms.

Rawls, Anne Warfield (ed.). *Interaction Orders of Everyday Life: Goffman's Contribution to Social Theory*. Routledge, 2023.

A recently edited volume revisiting Goffman's interaction order with new empirical and theoretical applications (e.g., in healthcare, digital communication, race, and gender).

Heritage, John. "Goffman, Garfinkel, and Conversation Analysis." In *Erving Goffman: Exploring the Interaction Order*, edited by Paul Drew and Anthony Wootton, Polity Press, 1988, pp. 92–130.

Shows how Goffman's ideas underpin conversation analysis and ethnomethodology—demonstrating the empirical robustness of the interaction order.

Extensions into Contemporary Contexts

Jacobsen, Michael Hviid. "Goffman in Cyberspace: Interaction, Ritual, and Self in the Digital Age." In *The Contemporary Goffman*, edited by Michael Hviid Jacobsen and Søren Kristiansen, Routledge, 2019, pp. 253–274.

Directly addresses whether the interaction order holds in digital environments—arguing that even online, users orient to Goffmanian norms (e.g., turn-taking, face-work, audience segregation).

Tillmann-Healy, Laurel M. "Goffman in the Internet Age: Revisiting the Interaction Order." *Symbolic Interaction*, vol. 43, no. 3, 2020, pp. 357–375.

Examines how digital platforms reshape—but do not eliminate—the interaction order, especially through context collapse and algorithmic mediation.

Mondada, Lorenza. "The Interaction Order: A Special Issue Introduction." *Journal of Pragmatics*, vol. 170, 2020, pp. 1–10.

Highlights the ongoing relevance of Goffman's framework in linguistic pragmatics, multimodal interaction, and embodied co-presence—even in mediated settings.

Theoretical Syntheses Linking Interaction Order to Broader Sociology

Collins, Randall. *Interaction Ritual Chains*. Princeton University Press, 2004.

While building his own theory, Collins explicitly credits Goffman's interaction order as the starting point for understanding how micro-interactions generate emotional energy, group solidarity, and social structure.

Alexander, Jeffrey C. *The Drama of Social Life: A Dramatur-*

gical Approach to Sociology. Routledge, 2019.

Revives Goffman's dramaturgy and interaction order as central to cultural sociology, showing how performance and ritual sustain collective life.

Critical but Constructive Engagements

Smith, Dorothy E. *Institutional Ethnography: A Sociology for People*. AltaMira Press, 2005.

While critical of Goffman's apolitical stance, Smith acknowledges that everyday interaction (the interaction order) is where institutional power becomes tangible—suggesting a fruitful synthesis.

Wacquant, Loïc. "Goffman's Place in Social Theory." In *Body & Soul: Notebooks of an Apprentice Boxer*, Oxford University Press, 2004, pp. 225–238.

Argues that Goffman's focus on the interaction order offers a crucial corrective to overly structural accounts—especially when studying embodiment and marginality.

Primary Works by Erving Goffman

Goffman, E. (1959). *The Presentation of Self in Everyday Life.* Doubleday.
— The foundational text where Goffman introduces the dramaturgical model using theatrical metaphors like "front stage", "backstage", and "performance".

Goffman, E. (1963). *Behaviour in Public Places.* Free Press.
— Explores how individuals manage impressions in public settings.

Goffman, E. (1967). *Interaction Ritual: Essays on Face-to-Face Behaviour.* Anchor Books.
— Expands on rituals and face-saving behaviours in social interaction.

Goffman, Erving. (1967). "On Face-Work: An Analysis of Ritual Elements in Social Interaction." In Interaction Ritual: Essays on Face-to-Face Behaviour, pp. 5–45. New York: Anchor Books.
— This foundational essay is essential. Goffman introduces the concept of "face" as a sacred, socially maintained image and shows how everyday interactions involve ritual practices

(e.g., apologies, greetings, excuses) to maintain mutual face and social harmony.

Goffman, Erving. (1967). "The Nature of Deference and Demeanour." In Interaction Ritual: Essays on Face-to-Face Behaviour, pp. 47–95. New York: Anchor Books.

— Here, Goffman expands his ritual framework by distinguishing between deference (respect shown to others) and demeanour (the impression of one's own worthiness). He argues these are ritualised performances that structure social hierarchy and mutual recognition in daily life.

Goffman, E. (1961). *Asylums: Essays on the Social Situation of Mental Patients and Other Inmates.* Anchor Books.

— Applies dramaturgical concepts to total institutions.

Goffman, Erving. (1963). *Stigma: Notes on the Management of Spoilt Identity.* Englewood Cliffs, NJ: Prentice-Hall. — This is Goffman's foundational text on stigma, where he introduces core concepts such as **discredited vs. discreditable identities**, **information control**, **passing**, **covering**, and the **moral career of the stigmatised person**. It remains the cornerstone of sociological and interdisciplinary work on stigma and identity.

Goffman, E. (1974). *Frame Analysis: An Essay on the Organization of Experience.* Harvard University Press.

— Builds on dramaturgy by analysing how people define and interpret social situations.

Goffman, E. (1977). The Arrangement Between the Sexes. Theory and Society, 4(3), 301–331.

— A lesser-known but essential article where Goffman directly theorises gender as a structural and interactional system of "ceremonial deference" and asymmetrical rituals.

Educational & Analytical Overviews

Doing Sociology (2022). *Erving Goffman's Dramaturgical Approach.*

A concise and accessible summary of Goffman's key ideas and their sociological significance.

EBSCO Research Starters. *Dramaturgical Analysis.*

Provides a scholarly overview and bibliography of dramaturgical theory.

Helpful Professor (2022). *Dramaturgical Analysis – Examples, Definition, Pros, Cons.*

Offers a student-friendly breakdown of the theory with examples and critiques.

ThoughtCo (2024). *Goffman's Front-Stage and Backstage Behaviour.*

Explains key dramaturgical concepts with real-life examples.

Fiveable (2024). *Goffman's Dramaturgical Approach.*

Connects dramaturgy to performance studies and symbolic interactionism.

www.ingramcontent.com/pod-product-compliance
Lightning Source LLC
Chambersburg PA
CBHW051526020426
42333CB00016B/1799